Decorative Tropical Fish

ESTHER J.J. VERHOEF-VERHALLEN

REBO
PRODUCTIONS

© 1997 Rebo Productions b.v., Lisse, The Netherlands
Published by Rebo Productions Ltd, 1998

text: Esther J.J. Verhoef-Verhallen
cover design: Ton Wienbelt, The Hague, The Netherlands
photographic editor: Marieke Uiterwijk
editor: Jacqueline Wouda
layout: Signia, Winschoten, The Netherlands
typesetting: Hof&Land Typografie, Maarssen, The Netherlands

editing, production and overall co-ordination:
TextCase Boekproducties, Groningen, The Netherlands

E0098UK
ISBN 1 901094 74 x

Contents

CHAPTER I

The history of aquarium fish keeping

Keeping ornamental fish as a hobby is nothing new. Fish were kept and bred thousands of years ago. They mainly served as food supplies, but later they were kept for their aesthetic value as well.

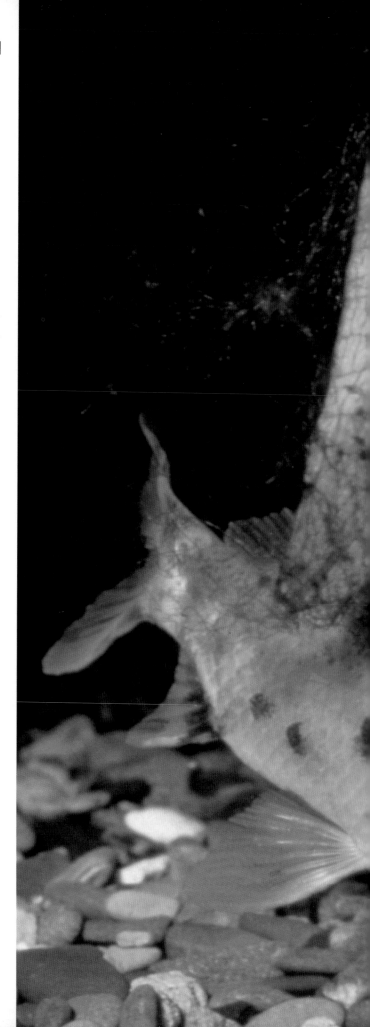

Many goldfish also existed hundreds of years ago.

The Romans

We know that the Romans kept fish in artificially created ponds. Not all fish were kept purely for their aesthetic value – this luxury was only set aside for exotic marine fish. Freshwater fish met with quite a different fate – they were seen as a food supply. The same distinction was made in the numerous public aquaria in the Roman Empire.

Nevertheless, it was very difficult for the Romans to keep marine fish alive at this time. The demands that the marine fish made on the water composition were high and practically impossible to meet for the inhabitants of inland cities away from the coast. Further inland, attractive freshwater fish were therefore the only ornamental fish that could be kept. The fish were kept both indoors and outdoors in ponds.

China

Thousands of years before our time, the Chinese kept silver crucian carp in large ponds. At first, their aesthetic qualities were deemed less important than their usefulness as a food source. They were reared and bred by the population of southern China and fish were regularly netted and eaten for supper the same day.

Comet goldfish shubunkin

Every so often, the Chinese would discover gold or orange coloured fish amongst the greyish-brown coloured carps. They considered these so special, that they kept them apart from the rest. The members of the nobility and the clergy mainly took care of these "golden chis", as they were known. From around the year 1000, more and more Chinese began to take up "chi" breeding. Special ponds were set up for the most beautiful fish, who were selected for colour and shape. Later these first goldfish were also kept in large, glass covered earthenware dishes, and in "dragon bowls", semi-transparent, specially made spherical pots – the very first fish bowls. Many of these were exported to Europe and were very much in vogue for a time.

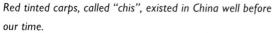

Red tinted carps, called "chis", existed in China well before our time.

Goldfish breeds

Not only the Chinese, but also the Japanese were very influential in the emergence of many variants of goldfish. In the 15th century, goldfish were regularly imported from China to Japan, where they very quickly settled down. The Japanese mainly applied themselves to breeding goldfish with deviant body forms. Such clearly *mis*formed fish have as many opponents as admirers.

It is often thought that these fish are the result of fashion whims in recent decades. Nothing could be less true. Goldfish breeds such as skygazers have existed for hundreds of years already. Because goldfish could only be seen from above at that time, the positioning of the eye on top of the head instead of at the side was considered very pretty.

Japan and the koi carp

About a thousand years ago, the nobility began to keep and breed stone carps in Japan. Little notice was taken at first if there was a fish in the pond with an unusual colour, but later these special carp, in parallel with goldfish breeding by the Chinese, were selected for their colour. It was only at the start of the 20th century, however, that the Japanese started to refine the body shape of these coloured carps and to define colour patterns.

A complete culture has been built up around these spectacularly coloured fish. The koi carp or "Nishikigoi", as they are called in Japan, are very highly regarded, and for the Japanese they embody the symbol of masculinity, love and steadfastness. Special standards early on described

Red cap veiltail

Koi carp come in many colours and patterns, but only a small number of them meet the high standards of the Japanese.

The picturesque beauty of a koi carp.

what the colours and colour distribution and the body shape of the ideal specimen of the diverse colour types should look like. These standards are still observed to this day.

Koi lovers claim that the best and most beautiful koi must be sought in Japan, and exorbitant prices are sometimes paid for high quality specimens. This is not so strange, given that the koi only arrived in Europe and the United States after the Second World War. Although they are now bred in large quantities all over the world, the Japanese have an advantage over the rest of the world that is difficult to overcome in terms of genetic knowledge and the recognition of truly beautiful fish.

The introduction of the aquarium in Europe

In the early 17th century, the first goldfish from China arrived in Europe via the merchant navy. These were still kept in dragon bowls and porcelain bowls at the time. Only halfway through the 19th century did Europeans begin to keep fish in glass bowls.

The first public aquarium was set up at London Zoo in the middle of the 19th century. Years later, other large cities in Europe followed the English example. Interested members of the public marvelled at the colourful splendour of the exotic water creatures that members of the merchant navy had brought back home with them from foreign travels. The bowls were placed amongst unfamiliar and spectacular plant varieties and

Koi carp

as the paradise fish and the swordtails, as well as the goldfish, were very popular at the beginning of the 20th century. These colourful fish species could adapt to fluctuations in temperature and water quality reasonably well and quickly. Later on, experiments were done with heating the water using oil lamps, but the results were not very satisfactory.

The guppy was one of the first aquarium fish in Europe.

Tropical fish are caught primitively.

miniature trees which were also brought back from all corners of the globe.

In those days owning fish and all manner of other exotic creatures and plant varieties was only possible for the upper classes. It was a long time before it would become possible for everyone to own an aquarium.

Technology

In the days when this hobby was still in its infancy, people were not able to keep all species of fish alive, since they had insufficient technical and scientific knowledge to keep the water in the aquaria at a suitable constant temperature. Many fishes also met an untimely death through the primitive methods of transport. For this reason, robust exotic fish such

The swordtail

Macropodus opercularis, *the paradise fish*

Keeping tropical fish could therefore only really take off once the technology became more reliable and more advanced, during the period following the Second World War. The equipment available to us today is so affordable and reliable that it really is possible for everyone to own an aquarium.

Imports

In former times, nearly all tropical fish were imported from the areas where they lived. Catching them in the wild was a necessary evil, since at that time there was insufficient knowledge and technology to persuade fish to breed in an aquarium. The fish were caught by the native population using the most primitive of methods, and many fish did not survive the catching process. The inadequate methods of transport also contributed to an untimely death for many fish. More than half of the fish failed to survive the journey over thousands of kilometres to their final destination. It is therefore not surprising that those concerned about animal rights were distressed by this capturing of fish, and were afraid that certain species of fish would die out in their natural biotopes.

Fortunately a lot has changed since then. Enthusiastic aquarists have succeeded in getting most species of fish to reproduce in artificial conditions, so that only a negligible number of fish need be caught in the wild. What is more, these species are so common in the wild that there is no question of them becoming extinct.

Most ornamental fish are still imported, though. The majority of these fish come from Asia, where vast numbers of ornamental fish are specially bred for annual export. The way in which fish are now transported is not comparable with the appalling conditions of the old days. The modern aquarist need not worry about the potential negative effects that may have been associated with his hobby in the past.

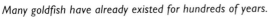

Many goldfish have already existed for hundreds of years.

Above: a female guppy

CHAPTER 2

Purchase, set-up and maintenance

There are choices to be made when buying an aquarium. The fish, the size and shape of the aquarium and how it is set up all depend on each other.

Most cichlids live in pairs.

The aquarium

Aquaria are made of two different materials these days – plastic and glass. A plastic aquarium has the disadvantage that it is less durable and does not remain attractive for as long, so most people opt for a glass aquarium.

The ideal size of an aquarium depends on a number of factors. The size and temperament of the fish kept in it are two of these, but the aquarium should of course also fit in with the space in which it is situated.

Budget considerations also play a role. With a large aquarium, not only the tank itself is more expensive, but equipment is also needed of a much higher capacity, which costs more to buy and uses up more electricity. More decorations, plants, pieces of bogwood and gravel will also be needed to decorate such a large aquarium. A smaller aquarium with accessories is therefore much cheaper to buy and the electricity bill also works out lower. On the other hand, the water composition in an aquarium that only holds a few litres is less stable, and caring for it takes up more time.

A rectangular aquarium

Irregularly shaped aquaria

There has never been such a range of aquarium shapes as there is now. Spherical aquaria, triangular, octagonal, and hexagonal aquaria, pyramid-shaped aquaria and tall, narrow column-shaped aquaria are only a few of the many aquaria shapes available. Not all shapes are suitable for all fish. Fish that like to swim a lot, for example, will definitely not have enough space in a narrow, tall aquaria to swim around happily.

Relatively few fish can be kept in most irregularly shaped aquaria. In the popular columnar and pyramid aquaria, for example, the water surface area is very small. As gases can only be exchanged, with the exception of oxygen, through the water surface, there may be too little oxygen for the fish. The larger the surface water area, the more varieties of fish can be kept in the aquarium. In practice, most people therefore opt for a classic, rectangular aquarium.

Purchase

Every aquarium centre offers a wide choice of new aquaria, but most aquarists start off with a – much cheaper – second-hand aquarium. Whether it is new or second-hand, an aquarium must first of all be tested for leaks. Aquaria which have been used and have then been empty for a while nearly always leak, as the glue holding them together has dried out. Leaks can also arise when transporting an aquarium. An aquarium must always be transferred when empty and as carefully as possible. Fluctuations in pressure must be avoided as far as possible. Before you set up an aquarium, you should test whether or not it leaks. Note that large leakages show up immediately after filling, while smaller ones are sometimes only noticeable after a few days.

If the aquarium leaks, empty it completely and make sure it is dry and clean. Scrape off old traces of algae and scale and remove all grease

Rineloricaria fallax

Above: algae-eaters such as this Gyrioncheilus aymonieri are ideal fish when too much algae grows on the root wood and the plants, but they do not feel at home in sparsely decorated tanks.

Below: Apistogramma nijsseni

from the glass. The old glue can be carefully removed with a razor blade. Then re-glue the aquarium with transparent glue. Make sure special glue for aquaria is used, for some types of glue can be poisonous for fish.

The base

Small aquaria can often sit very nicely on a cupboard or table, but you will need a special base for larger aquaria. There are many different types of bases for sale, in all sorts of shapes, colours and materials, but you can of course always make one yourself. Make sure that the construction is sturdy enough to take the weight of the aquarium, the water and the gravel. There must be enough room below or next to the aquarium for the equipment and all the other items associated with the aquarium. These can be hidden behind a little door.

Make sure the base is level and the floor on the which the support rests is stable. Wooden floors which move with every footstep should be strengthened first. To absorb small changes in pressure, place a layer of polystyrene foam about one centimetre thick between the base and the aquarium.

Algae-eaters carry out good work in very algal aquaria.

Location

An aquarium should always be situated in a dark spot well away from the light from outdoors. Direct sunlight almost always leads to an explosion of green algae. The less serious type of algae growth takes place directly on the glass and can be removed easily, but too much sunlight often results in the aquarium water turning green and turbid, and this type of algae growth cannot be brought under control. Also, plants have a tendency to grow towards the (sun)light, and that looks ugly if the window is beside or even behind the aquarium. Neither should an aquarium be placed next to a door. Finally, make sure that there are enough earthed power points in the direct vicinity of the aquarium, so that the equipment can be connected safely. You will always need at least three power points for an average tropical aquarium – one for the lighting, one for the pump and one for the heating element.

A good start is half the work – buy your fish at a specialist's.

The back wall

There are various types of back walls. In the aquarium centre you will find coloured back walls made of polystyrene with a textured surface. These are attached between the side walls on the inside of the aquarium. There are also backgrounds which are attached to the back of the aquarium. This type of background can be bought in different designs in any aquarium centre. You can also make the aquarium opaque by painting the back. Do not use ordinary paint for this – use school blackboard paint.

Rockeries

Rockeries are – provided that they are well arranged – not only pretty to look at, but they also offer a refuge for shyer fish which are active at night. The stones which are bought from the aquarium centre are not always cheap, which leads many people to the idea of collecting them themselves or buying them in a garden centre. If you want to do this, you should note that not all types of stones can be used in an aquarium. Many types give off substances, such as metal and calcium, which can have a negative effect on the water composition.

The stones that you buy in an aquarium shop are more or less safe for your fish. If you want to get your stones elsewhere, restrict yourself to slate and lava, granite, basalt, quartz and river pebbles. Stone types such as marble, limestone, chalk and sandstone must be avoided at all costs. Shells, corals and sea sand also do not

Paracheirodon axelrodi

belong in a freshwater aquarium. Wash the stones carefully before inserting and boil them in clean water for an hour if possible.

By arranging the rocks and stones to create caves and terraces, you can give the aquarium more depth, as well as creating refuges for the fish. Never stack the stones loosely on one another. They can topple through vibrations and the

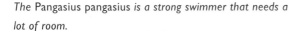

The Pangasius pangasius *is a strong swimmer that needs a lot of room.*

Nannochromis transvestitus, *a small cichlid*

In an aquarium with cichlids, the rocks must be well stuck down to prevent the fish from digging them up.

consequences of a crack in the glass bottom of the aquarium are unimaginable. Larger fish, especially cichlids, like to dig in the bottom.

They can dig up rockeries doing this with all the disastrous consequences that this entails. Therefore always put the stones directly on the bottom, not on the gravel, and glue them firmly together using transparent aquarium glue.

Root wood

Root wood

Stones and rocks can be combined well with root wood. Root wood is not only very decorative, it also provides hiding places for fry, and catfish love to hide under it or suck on the wood (when it is covered with algae).

To give the wood a more natural appearance, you can attach ferns or moss to it. One big disadvantage of root wood is that it can give off orange dye in the water, even after it has been carefully brushed clean and boiled for a long time. For this reason, it is first dried out after the cleaning and boiling, and then coated with a layer of epoxy resin or polyurethane varnish. No more discoloration of the water will occur after this treatment.

Give the aquarium more depth by filling up the spaces behind the root wood and the stones with gravel.

The substrate

In a aquarium containing vegetation, a nutrient base must placed under the gravel. This is because gravel, particularly when it is still very clean and new, does not contain enough nutrients for the plants. A substrate with too many nutrients isn't good, either, since this will stimulate root growth and prevent the visible part of the plant from growing. Too heavy a nutrient base can also cause the roots to rot. The nutrient base should therefore be mixed with lava dust to create more air. Across this, spread a generous layer of gravel. Do not be too mean here, since the gravel prevents the nutrient base from coming into direct contact with the aquarium water, which will make the aquarium look like a muddy puddle.

Wash the gravel carefully in a bucket under fast running water. Only when the water is crystal clear is the gravel clean enough to be used. Gravel comes in all colours and sizes, but the most suitable varieties are the finer and smooth types. Many fish like to dig around in the bottom, and if the gravel has sharp edges they can

Root wood provides a hiding place for many types of fish.

Following pages: Corydoras species like to burrow in the bottom and a sandy bottom is very suitable for this.

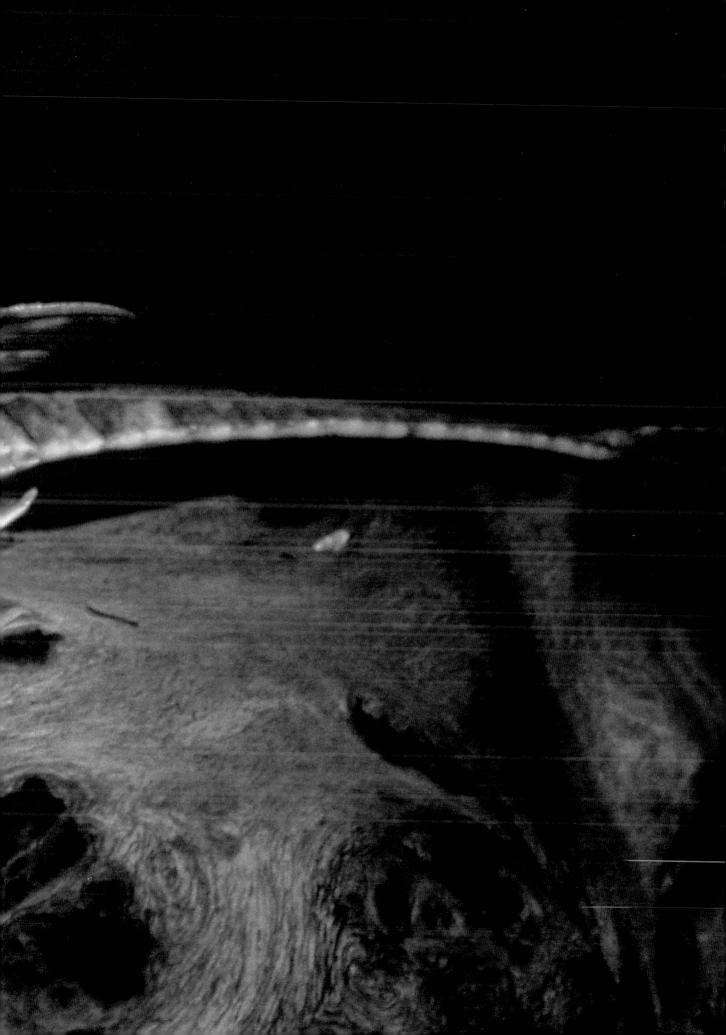

The Pristella maxillaris *is a shoaling fish.*

cut themselves. It is best to use dark-coloured gravel. Light-coloured gravel reflects against the stomachs of the fish and makes them look paler. If the layer of gravel is thicker towards the back of the aquarium, this gives a more attractive effect than if the layer of gravel is equally distributed.

Fill the gaps between the back wall and the rocks and root wood with gravel. If you are keeping fish species like the corydoras, or fish which like to bury themselves in the bottom, you should partly cover the bottom with well-washed sand. This sand can be kept in a glazed earthenware pot which is buried in the gravel.

This Telmatherina ladigesi *is an active and peaceful shoaling fish.*

The water

Before the equipment and plants are introduced you can fill the aquarium up to about halfway with water. Neither plants nor fish can tolerate tap water. This contains chlorine and metals which are not dangerous to people, but even very small quantities can be fatal to more vulnerable fish and plants.

Tap water must therefore be treated first. There are various products on sale which bind the metals in the water and neutralise the chlorine. Always let the water run indirectly into the aquarium using a plate or a saucer, so that the bottom is not stirred up.

Corydoras *species like to burrow.*

Filters

Filtering the aquarium water is necessary not only to keep the water clear, but an effective filter will also keep the quantity of invisible waste materials within limits.

The capacity of the filter must be in accordance with the size of the aquarium, and also the type of inhabitants. If we keep fish with a good appetite, who also like to burrow and dig in the bottom, a fairly strong filter will be necessary. A filter with too low a capacity will not sufficiently filter the water, allowing dangerous substances to accumulate and leading to a water environment where poisonous ammonia and nitrates gain the upper hand. That is very unhealthy for the fish and can even be deadly in some cases.

Botia macracantha, *clown loach*

Hemigrammoptersius caudalis

There are various ways of filtering the aquarium and there are also many different systems. Always make sure that the filter that you buy has sufficient capacity. Ask your specialist for advice about this, since the capacity required often depends on the actual type of filter.

Hyphessobrycon loretoensis

Glossolepis incisus

Heating

Tropical fish thrive best in water temperatures between 22 and 28°C. The water temperature must be kept constant for most fish. Fluctuations in temperature lead to stress and reduced resistance, which can make the fish ill. There are various systems on sale which can be used to heat the water. The best are the elements that are a heater and thermostat in one. These are available in different wattages.

Which element you should choose not only depends on the quantity of water to be heated, but also on the place where the aquarium is situated and the degree of insulation. In an aquarium with a cover, situated in a warm room, the temperature is maintained for longer than in an open tank in a cold room. In the first case about half a watt per litre is more than enough, but in the second case, one watt is necessary for each litre of water. Most heating combinations will break down if a part of them is out of the water.

Because aquarium water evaporates, the safest place for a heating element is a few centimetres from the bottom. Place the heating element as horizontally as possible in the aquarium, in order to make the best possible use of the rising heat. A heating element must never come into contact with plants, decorations or the substrate.

Lighting

A tropical aquarium must always be artificially lit, because tropical fish and plants are used to twelve to fourteen hours of sunlight a day. If the aquarium is lit dimly or not at all, the plants and fish will become diseased as a result. Such underlit aquaria are also plagued by unsightly brown algae. There are various systems used to light the aquarium, but neon tubes are best. These give off good light, last a long time and use relatively little electricity. Naturally the fitting must be resistant to water splashes, so it should only be bought at an aquarium centre. The light

given off by a 25 to 30 watt neon tube is enough for a tank 60cm wide, maximum. If the aquarium is wider than 60 cm or deeper than 40 cm, multiple tubes must be used alongside each other. Always put the neon tube at the front of the aquarium so that the shadow falls behind the fish and plants.

There are various types of neon tubes. The lamps that spread a purplish light are meant to illuminate the colours of the fish better, but do not provide enough light for plants to grow. Other neon tubes can be bought for this purpose.

The different types of neon lighting can be placed alongside one another without any problem. If you attach each neon tube to a separate switch and timer, you can create an artificial twilight

Gyrinocheilus aymonieri

Arius seemani

and in this way get a better view of the nocturnal fish in your aquarium in the evening. The aquarium lighting also must never be switched off suddenly.

Plants

It is best not to skimp on the number of plants when setting up a new aquarium. A tank with plenty of vegetation is not only attractive to look at, but the rich vegetation also prevents uncontrollable algae growth. This is because all the nutrients in the aquarium are absorbed by the plants, which does not give the algae a chance to multiply. Get some good advice at the aquarium centre on the care requirements of the plants, or get information from the literature.

Like fish, not all plants come from the same biotope and one type will grow and develop better in acid water, while another will slowly die off in the same water. The water hardness of the tap water can vary in different areas. A simple water test, which is available from the aquarium centre, or a telephone call to the water company, will soon provide the answer. Plants such as the *Lobelia cardinalis, Lysimachia nummularia* and most *cryprocorynes* are examples of hardy plant species which nearly always do well.

Arranging plants

There are a number of rules of thumb for arranging plants successfully. For example, large or fast-growing plants are always planted at the back or along the edges of the aquarium, and medium-sized ones in the middle. Small plants belong in the middle or at the front. Some plants do better when planted together in a clump, whilst others, such as the Amazon sword plant, are strictly solitary plants. Try to create as many contrasts in colour and shape as possible. To achieve this, place large-leafed plants next to small-leafed ones and light green plants next to dark green varieties. Also try to be a asymmetrical as possible. Eye-catching plants for example, are better not placed in the centre, but slightly to the left or right of centre. Foreground plants will look better planted in a diagonal line towards the back rather than right next to one another, parallel to the front of the tank. Remove any wires, elastic bands and pots from the plants and also any rotting leaves and stalks before you place the plants in the substrate.

Do not release fish straight away

Once all the plants have been arranged, the aquarium is completely filled and the equipment is attached, observe a rest period of about a month before you release the fish. During this

Arrange plants asymmetrically as far as possible – this is more attractive than when they are kept 'in rows'.

Corydorus

time, you should regularly check that the equipment is working, but this rest period also has another much more important role. The balance in the aquarium is still very unstable and there are still no bacteria present which can break down the excreta produced by the fish. If fish are released into the aquarium at this critical time, waste substances will build up at a tremendous rate.

This high quantity of harmful substances in the water will lead to outbreaks of disease and finally to mass fish deaths, the so-called "new aquarium syndrome". Only after a month can you release a couple of robust fish, but definitely wait another two weeks before you buy the rest of the fish.

Different fish species

Buying fish is one of the best parts of the hobby for many aquarists. Particularly in better stocked aquarium centres, there are so many different fish for sale that it is not only very difficult to

make a responsible choice, but also not to buy too many fish at once. In both cases, do not make this well-known beginner's mistake. Overpopulation is the root of many problems. Try and confine yourself to buying a relatively small quantity of healthy and strong fish, which all have the same requirements in terms of water composition and temperature, and can live

Shoaling fish like these cardinal tetras need to have many others of their own species around them. A little shoal should consist of at least five, but preferably more of the same species.

This predator, the Hepsetus odoe, *cannot be kept in a community aquarium.*

together in harmony. It goes without saying that you should not buy just one of a species that should be kept in a shoal, or a shoal of fish which prefer to live a solitary life. Small fish which are rather shy will be forced into the vegetation by fast swimming fish species, and fish that are aggressive do not belong in an aquarium with small, peaceful fish.

Also make sure you buy fish that live in different water zones. This way they will not disturb one another when swimming. If you want to buy several varieties of shoaling fish, then buy species which are very different in terms of colour, body shape and swimming style. That will create a balanced and harmonious overall effect. You can get sound advice at a good aquarium centre, but you can of course learn a lot about the temperament and requirements of the different species of fish through reading a lot about them, or by talking to experienced aquarists.

Baryancistrus *spec.* L91

Fish like Pterophyllum altum *and the* Discus *are sensitive species. They are therefore not suitable for new aquarists.*

Sick and healthy fish

Make sure the fish are healthy at the time of purchase. Never buy fish from badly maintained, algae-covered, cloudy aquaria. The fish may indeed still look healthy in such conditions, but under the influence of stress (transport and their new environment), their resistance breaks down and they can soon become sick.

For the same reason, do not buy fish from tanks containing visibly sick or even dead fish. Other symptoms of disease are compression of the fins, an irregular swimming style or obvious listlessness and damage or tumours on the skin or fins.

The red-nosed tetra is found in South America.

Also do not buy fish with protruding scales, or which breathe too quickly or constantly rub against stones or plants. Although a lot of research has been done on fish disease and there are many effective medicines on the market, there are still many diseases for which little or nothing can be done. A particular bacteria or fungus can contaminate the whole aquarium population in no time at all, with all the consequences this entails.

Transport

During transport home, temperature fluctuations should be kept to a minimum. Most shopkeepers also wrap the bags in a thick layer of newspaper which, due to its insulating effect, keeps the water temperature reasonably constant. Do not immediately release the fish into the aquarium. First lay the transport bag on the aquarium water for a quarter of an hour to remove the inevitable difference in water temperature. After this, carefully open the bag at the top and tip some water from the aquarium into the transport bags to make the transfer to another water composition as gradual as possible for the fish. Make sure that the bags do not flap shut at the top,

for then the fish will quickly suffocate. Let the opened bags float about on the surface of the water for a quarter of an hour after this.

In most cases, the water in the transport bag will already be contaminated by fish excreta, so try to prevent the transport water from ending up in the aquarium water. Scoop the fish out of the transport bags with a net and carefully release them into the aquarium. Do not feed the fish on

A shoal of sumatrans.

Microglanis iheringi

Panaque suttoni

the first day. Do not tap on the glass to make them move; it is important to let them adjust to their new living environment in peace.

Maintenance

If the correct equipment for the size of the aquarium is installed, and not too many fish are kept in it, an aquarium does not need much maintenance. To avoid contamination of the water, you should feed the fish moderately. If food flakes are used, 2 to 3 flakes of food a day are more than enough for a fish about 5 cm long. Most fish receive much more food than this, with the result that a large quantity is not eaten up and sinks to the bottom where it rots. The golden rule is therefore to give little food, and this will certainly cause no problems with high quality food. Daily maintenance means nothing more than checking the water temperature and counting the fish. Dead and sick fish should be removed from the aquarium immediately, since they are a source of infection for the other aquarium inhabitants.

About once a month you should set aside a few hours for the periodical maintenance of the aquarium. Any algae on the front of the aquarium can be removed with a sponge, or carefully – avoiding scratches on the glass – using a razor blade. If the plants are doing very well and some are growing exceptionally fast, and beginning to take over, you can thin them out or cut off their

Tateurndina ocellicauda

tops. Siphoning up the dirt (and some of the water) is best done with a piece of garden hose which you only use for the aquarium. Changing the water should be done once every other month, and the filter equipment should be cleaned at the same time.

Make sure that all the bits and pieces that you use, such as sponges and buckets, are only used for the aquarium and not for anything else.

Rachoviscus crassiceps

CHAPTER 3

Catfish

There are many different types of catfish. They come from almost all over the world and both cold water and tropical species are known. Most catfish are nocturnal, peaceful vegetarians or omnivores who live on or close to the bottom.

Corydoras *species come in all sorts of colours and patterns.*

What are catfish?

The catfish order is distinguished from the others in that they have no scales. For protection, many catfish are entirely or partially covered with bony plates, but there are also completely naked catfish. All catfish are able to take in oxygen via the intestines or stomach as well as by breathing through the gills, and some species even absorb oxygen through their skin.

Mailed catfish

The mailed catfish family, known under the scientific name *Callichthyidae*, are mainly found in the extensive rainforests of the Amazon region. These fish feel at home in pleasantly warm, gently flowing water along the densely vegetated banks of rivers and small lakes. They

conceal themselves amongst the foliage from large predators, and they are also not seen so easily by fish-eating birds.

Although the water in which a number of these fish live is usually reasonably clean, nature has provided them with a specific adaptation that makes it easy for them to survive in water that is highly polluted and is therefore low in oxygen.

Corydoras, *albino variety*

Corydoras *enjoy the company of several of the same species.*

Hoplosternum thoracatum

Corydoras aeneus *is the best-known armoured catfish.*

This is that the fish can take in oxygen by taking air from above the water. The oxygen from the air which is swallowed is absorbed through the intestines and the gills then pass the carbon dioxide out again. In this way they can also survive on dry land for a short time. Since mailed catfish usually do not obtain enough oxygen by breathing through their gills, these fish must definitely be given the chance to breathe above water, or they will suffocate. All mailed catfish are shoaling fish. In the wild, they sometimes form shoals containing hundreds of same species, and they seek out each other's company in the aquarium, too. Fish that belong to this family are predominantly nocturnal, which means that they only go in search of food towards dusk. An exception is the *Corydoras* genus.

The *Corydoras* genus is the largest genus of mailed catfish, and these fish have been incredibly popular aquarium fish for many years. Almost two hundred different species are known and new species are constantly being imported, which all differ from one another in markings and colours. *Corydoras* are small shoaling fish and must never be kept alone or in too small a group. Depending on the species, they grow to between 3 and 7 cm long.

These catfish are particularly suitable for the community aquarium, which need not be large,

Hoplosternum pectorale

Other well-known mailed catfish are those in the *Hoplosternum* genus. These friendly fish grow to between 15 and 20 cm long. They can survive in nearly all water types, even in polluted water, without seeming to suffer any ill effects. As these species of fish grow very large and enjoy a very active lifestyle, they definitely require a lot of room. A community aquarium at least 80 cm wide will provide a suitable home for three to five of these creatures.

Armoured catfish

but must have enough refuges. They thrive very well in the most diverse water types, and will eat almost anything, from dry flakes and tablets to small live food. As fish from this genus like to dig in the bottom, rough or sharp gravel is not ideal as substrate. The bottom must consist entirely or partially of washed sand. You can also bury a dish filled with washed sand in the gravel. This can serve as a good feeding place. If the shell is situated in a sheltered part of the aquarium, for example, under overhanging plants near some bogwood or stones, the fish will very quickly feel at home there. *Corydoras* species are peaceful and active fish which tend to keep to themselves. They leave the other fish in the aquarium in peace.

Most catfish of the armoured catfish *(Loricariidae)* family are highly suitable and very popular aquarium fish. These fish owe their name to the strong bony plates which cover them. Armoured catfish come from the northern part of South America, including the Amazon area. There they mainly live in fast-flowing mountain rivers rich in oxygen. With their powerful sucker-like mouth, they attach themselves firmly to the stones so that they are not carried away by the current.

These catfish also like a fast current in the aquarium. The aquarium water must be crystal clear, as these fish are not very resistant to

Sturisoma aureum

Ancistrus dolichopterus

Rineloricaria sp.

under plant roots. Armoured catfish which are kept in the aquarium are no exception to this and therefore you should only feed these fish towards the evening.

Armoured catfish are vegetarians. They are very keen on algae, which they neatly scrape off plants, bogwood and the aquarium glass.

If the aquarium contains insufficient algae or none at all, then these fish must definitely be fed on crushed vegetarian food tablets or blanched lettuce or spinach.

contaminated or turbid water. All armoured catfish are creatures that only actively go in search of food towards dusk and in the evening. During the day they hide among the foliage and

One of the most striking armoured catfish, only discovered very recently, is *Hypancistrus zebra*. This is a fish with a striking colour pattern that is about 8 cm long.

Due to its striking and attractive appearance, it

Hypancistrus zebra

Sturisoma Aureum

has won many fans all over the world in a very short time. These fish can live as solitaries, but if there is enough space and refuges, there will be no problem with keeping several zebras together. Other striking aquarium inhabitants which are among the group of armoured catfish are *Panaque nigrolineatus* and *Panaque sutto-*

ni. In contrast to the *Hypancistrus zebra*, these fish look anything but friendly. However, underneath that frightening appearance there is a peaceful fish that wouldn't harm a fly and keeps to itself. They live exclusively on algae and are therefore difficult to keep in newly set up aquaria. In their natural biotope, in Colombia

Baryancistrus *sp.* L91

Pseudacanthicus leopardus

Peckoltia vittata

Panaque nigrolineatus

amongst other places, they can grow quite large, but in the aquarium they rarely exceed 20 cm. Like all armoured catfish, these fish also make few demands on the water composition, but if you want to keep them healthy the water must definitely be clear and rich in oxygen.

Pseudacanthicus leopardus   *Following pages:* Panaque suttoni

Butterfly catfish

All catfish have one or several pairs of mouth feelers which they use in the dark to search for food, but no other catfish has such amazingly long ones as the butterfly catfish.

Butterfly catfish also have no scales or bony plates. They come from Mexico and the northern part of South America, where they are found in various types of water. They are active and amusing bottom dwellers who keep themselves hidden by day and only show their face a little at dusk. Most butterfly catfish are harmless fish, but this genus also produces some real predators.

Well-known aquarium fish which are butterfly catfish (scientific name *Pimelodidae)*, and which other fish need not fear, include the

Pimelodus ornatus *is a butterfly catfish.*

large *Pimelodus ornatus* and the friendly *Microglanis iheringi,* only 6 cm long.

Pimelodus ornatus
Below: Microglanis iheringi

Bearded catfish

Bearded catfish, known under the scientific name *Mochocidae,* come from Africa. There they live in small groups in various types of water, both in large rivers and shallow pools. Bearded catfish are nocturnal fish. Although they are not really shoaling fish in the true sense of the word, they do like to live together with others of the same species.

A few fish from this family are well-known aquarium fish, in particular the upside-down catfish *(Synodontis nigriventris).* This fish from the Republic of Congo grows to about 10 cm

Synodontis reboli

long. It is an active and good-natured fish which mainly goes in search of food in the evening and lives in the central and lower zones. The most striking feature of this species is that the crea-

Synodontis nigriventis *always swims upside-down.*

tures swim upside-down. Young upside-down catfish swim belly down, but they assume the swimming position of their parent fish increasingly frequently until eventually they only swim on their back. They like somewhat softer, and preferably rather acidic, water with a temperature of between 23 and 26°C, but they can also adapt to water that is a little harder. These fish really appreciate refuges.

Bearded catfish which only occasionally swim upside-down are the *Synodontis angelicus* and the *Synodontis schoutendeni*. We do not come across these catfish with their striking colours in aquaria as much as the upside-down catfish, which is probably due to the fact that these fish can grow to nearly twice the size. Nevertheless, they are a great asset to any large community aquarium with their splendid markings and

Synodontis angelicus

Synodontis schoutendeni

lively behaviour. The substrate should not be too sharp in this aquarium, as the fish will hurt themselves on it whilst looking for food. Both species need plenty of vegetarian food. If they are not given it, they will definitely nibble on feathery-leafed plants.

Aspredinidae

The catfish which are known internationally by the scientific name *Aspredinidae* are sometimes given other and more humorous names. The fish belonging to this family are perhaps the strangest of the catfish family. Their appearance is initially reminiscent of a dead leaf, and that is precisely the intention.

These fish mainly live in shallow water in the rainforests of South America. They stay hidden by day on, or even in, the bottom, amongst piles of dead leaves, and are not easily noticed by their enemies due to their camouflage and body shape. Only towards the evening do they go in search of food. All the catfish in this family have intensive brood care characteristics, but they are rarely bred in the aquarium.

One well-known catfish that does well in the aquarium is the *Bunocephalus coracoideus*, the

Bunocephalus coracoides

Eutropiellus debauwi

banjo catfish. This is about 13 cm long and eats small live food, but also nibbleson food tablets. It likes to hide by day in the aquarium, behaving just like its family members in the wild. We are not able to provide a thick layer of dead leaves in the aquarium. Not just because this doesn't look nice, but also because the biological balance in the aquarium is not the same as in the wild. The water will quickly become acidic and cloudy in the confines of the aquarium. This catfish likes a substrate of good, well washed sand where it can burrow. A powerful motor filter is necessary to keep the aquarium water clean where these fish are kept.

Eurasian catfish

Not all catfish have a so-called "low-level" suction mouth and a flat stomach. The Euro-Asian catfish family (or *Siluridae),* for example, contains a much-loved aquarium fish whose

Kryptopterus bicirrhis

body shape is different from that of most catfish. This is the Indian glass catfish *(Kryptopterus bicirrhis),* a peaceful shoaling fish which feels at home in a large, moderately lit aquarium with peaceful neighbours. A dark substrate, dense peripheral vegetation and some floating plants will also be greatly appreciated by these fish. Indian glass catfish are practically transparent. They grow to about 13 cm long and prefer to live in the central and lower zones. This variety is found on certain Indonesian islands and in Thailand and Malaysia. These fish like to eat small live food, but also accept food flakes.

Glass catfish (Schilbeidae)

Glass catfish also differ significantly in body shape from most other catfish. They are also active during the day rather than at dusk and night-time.

They come from certain parts of Africa and South East Asia. This small family of fish includes the well-known African aquarium fish, *Eutropiellus debauwi* and *Eutropiellus buffei.* These two fish look very similar. They are shoaling fish who must definitely be kept alongside others of the same species. They are very atractive fish which like lots of movement in the water, so that they can swim against the current.
This species is easy to care for. They eat almost anything and are not very sensitive to the water composition, although soft and slightly acidic water is ideal for them.

CHAPTER 4

Livebearing fish

Livebearing fish have been popular as aquarium fish for many years. A number of them are suitable fish for beginners, which can feel at home in any aquarium and are easy to breed. They are known for their dazzling colours and lively character.

Guppies now come in countless colours and varieties.

Ovoviparous and livebearing fish

Scientists distinguish between two large groups of fish which give birth to live young. One group is known as 'livebearing', and the other is called 'ovoviparous'. In the first group the embryo is linked to its mother by an umbilical cord. In ovoviparids, the group which covers most well-known aquarium fish, there is no contact at all between the mother and the embryos. The eggs are fertilised internally by the male and the female bears the eggs until the fry are large enough. Then they burst out of the egg and swim out into the world. We will only discuss ovoviparids here, since they include many very well-known and popular aquarium fish.

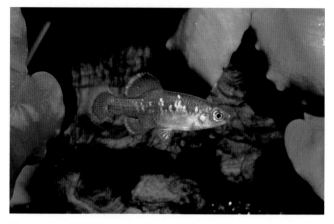

Zoogoneticus quitzeoensis *is live-bearing.*

Reproduction

Ovoviparous fish are able to produce several batches of eggs after mating only once. After the eggs have been fertilised by several males, they can also give birth to fry from different fathers in the same batch. How many fry the female will produce and how much time elapses between the batches depends not only on the type of fish but also on other factors such as quality of nutrition, environmental temperature and age.

Normally a female gives birth to between ten and eighty fry, which are immediately able to take care of themselves. Since they are so small, other fish see them as a welcome addition to their diet, and the mother will also sometimes eat her own offspring, although she will be more likely to do

this in a small, overpopulated aquarium than if there is enough space. The fry swim away immediately after birth and seek cover amongst dense vegetation. There they eat small live food and algae until they have grown larger and can join the adult fish.

It is very easy to determine the sex of fish belonging to the large ovoviparous group. In all the males the anal fin has been transformed into a mating organ. This is called the 'gonopodium' in these fish. The halfbeaks are an exception to this rule. Their reproductive organ is called an 'andropodium'.

Poeciliidae

The best-known family of ovoviparous fish is the *Poeciliidae* family. These are not real shoaling fish like neon tetras or zebra danios, but they do like each other's company. These fish are therefore never kept as a pair, but usually in a small group. The males are active lovers and sometimes chase the females all day long. This is why more females than males are usually kept in the aquarium. This allows the females to 'relieve' each other from time to time.

Poeciliidae are active, lively fish which occupy all zones of the aquarium. They are very adaptable and feel perfectly comfortable in most community aquaria. The water composition is not particularly important, although most of them do prefer water to which some iodine free

Guppies are viviparous. This female has just given birth to young.

salt has been added. This is because they are not only found in fresh water in the wild, but also in brackish water. The natural range of these fish is restricted to the southern United States, Central America and northern South America. The *Poeciliidae* family includes the guppy, the swordtail and the platy.

Female guppy, long-finned variant.

The Poecilia *genus*

The most popular of the whole large group of ovoviparous fish is the guppy, whose scientific name is *Poecilia reticulata*. The colourful guppies with their long fins, which we can see and admire in aquarium centres, are special variants which do not occur in the wild. The original guppy is a much smaller fish, grey-beige in colour with a short, rounded tail. The males have colourful touches on their dorsal fin, tail

Male 'double sword' guppy

Since guppies have been released in various areas to combat the larvae of the malaria mosquito, they can now also be found in other parts of the world. The speed and effectiveness with which they destroy malaria mosquito larvae has earned them the nickname 'mosquito fish'.

and body, but their colouring cannot be compared with the guppies which are bred today.

Wild guppies are extremely hardy fish which can easily adapt to the most difficult circumstances. They are found in both fresh and brackish water, and small shoals of these lively fish have also been reported in seawater. They originate from Barbados, Trinidad and Venezuela.

The variants are rather more sensitive and need more care than their tough relatives in the wild. They do best in medium to hard water with added salt and a temperature between 25 and 28°C.

Another fish which belongs to this group is *Poecilia Sphenops* or Black Molly. This fish grows to about 6cm long. As in the case of the guppy, the greyish-blue original form of the

The result of crossing black Mollies and giant sailfin mollies can only be seen in aquaria. These varieties do not breed with each other in the wild.

Wild-caught guppies

Poecilia Sphenops, the Black Molly. Male above, female below.

Poecilia velifera, *Sailfin Molly, male*

black Molly is virtually unknown, while almost every enthusiast knows or has once kept the velvet-black variant. Black Mollies are lively and friendly aquarium fish which do very well in the community aquarium. The disadvantage of these striking fish is that they quickly become ill if subjected to temperature fluctuations or stress. They need warm water, at a temperature of at least 26°C, in order to feel comfortable, and will also appreciate a good dash of iodine free salt in the aquarium water. In addition to dry food and all types of live food, this fish enjoys algae and other vegetable foods. The giant of the *Poecilia* genus is the sailfin molly, which carries the scientific name *Poecilia velifera*. Sailfin Mollies

can grow to more than 15cm long and the males are particularly noticeable because of their huge dorsal fin. The Sailfin Molly and the Black Molly will readily cross-breed in captivity, which is a good reason never to keep these fish together in an aquarium. It is not easy to breed Sailfin Mollies. Fry are born as regularly as clockwork, but the problem is that their growth often stagnates and the male's large dorsal fin does not always develop to its full size. In order to ensure that the fry will grow properly, plenty of space and a current in the water are necessary.

A good supply of vegetable food, particularly algae, plus a few tablespoonfuls of iodine free salt in the aquarium water are a necessity.

Xiphophorus helleri, *a long-finned variant.*

Male Sailfin Mollies have a huge sail-like fin which they display to frighten off other males and impress females.

Sailfin Mollies, just like Black Mollies, are sensitive to fluctuations in temperature; the correct water temperature for these fish is between 26 and 28°C. If the water temperature is outside this range, they will lose a lot of weight and judder about until they eventually die. Sailfin Mollies are now bred in many different colours.

Xiphophorus helleri

The Xiphophorus *genus*

The *Xiphophorus* genus forms another group of ovoviparous fish. These fish are found in the wild in the eastern part of Central America. Although the different varieties will cross-breed in the aquarium, researchers say that this does not happen in the wild. The explanation for this

is probably that in captivity the fish do not always have access to the right partner. Fish of the *Xiphophorus* genus come in countless different colours and patterns. Many of these variants have come into being through cross-breeding.

One very popular aquarium fish in this genus is *Xiphophorus Maculatus*, better known as the platy. These fish grow just 5cm long. Platys are very suitable fish for beginners. They can be kept in small aquaria and provide cheerful and colourful company.

Platys are bred in a huge number of different colours and patterns. The coral platy, with its plain deep red colour, is one of the best-known. The wagtail platy with its red body and black fins is also popular. Platys has now also been bred with a high dorsal fin, and these are called Simpson platys.

Not all platys are bred by enthusiasts, and various different colours occur in their original habitats in Mexico and Honduras. Platys are not fussy eaters. They can remain healthy throughout their lives on dry food, but they do like to eat some algae and live food. A water temperature of 23 to 25°C is ideal.

The swordtail (*Xiphophorus Helleri*) can grow to about 15cm in length. This fish owes its name to the fact that the lower fin ray of the tail is considerably lengthened. The original form of the swordtail comes from Mexico and Guatemala, where it lives in crystal-clear fast-running mountain streams and in swampy, almost stagnant pools.

Swordtails are hardy and will do well in a community aquarium. Since the males need a lot of space for their displays, a small aquarium is not very suitable for these fish, and they do not belong in a tank with vegetation which is too dense either. They are usually friendly towards

Next page: this is a particularly attractive variant of Xiphophorus variatus.

Swordtail (Xiphophorus helleri) *variant*

Below: swordtail, variant

Below: platys come in many different colours.

The original swordtail is known as the 'white' or 'green' swordtail.

other aquarium dwellers, but the males are sometimes rather intolerant.

Swordtails are very productive. A female can bring eighty fry into the world in a single batch. The development of the males is quite variable. Some of them can be identified as males fairly quickly, as they demonstrate the characteristic 'sword'. Others do not develop until they are older. The latter group grow to a much larger size than their fast-developing brothers, which will always be slimmer and more elegant.

Swordtails come in many different colours, and as with the platy a high-finned variant has also been bred, which is known as the Simpson swordtail. In the lyre-tailed swordtail the outer fin rays of all the fins are elongated. This variant is very beautiful and decorative, but unfortunately it is not very easy to breed these fish successfully.

This is because the gonopodium is also elongated in the males, which makes reproduction difficult or virtually impossible.

The platy does not grow very large and is a pleasant and lively fish.

The *Xiphophorus Variatus* is the third well-known aquarium fish of the *Xiphophorus* genus. At first sight this variant seems to be a cross between the swordtail and the platy, but it is a separate species which is also found in the wild. These fish grow to about six centimetres long.

Several variants are known, but the plain colours which we find in the swordtail and the platy do not occur in these colourful fish. These fish are highly suitable for beginners. They do well in community aquaria and they are particularly peaceful and lively.

Halfbeaks

There are several types of halfbeaks, and not all of them are livebearing, but the members of the small *Hemirhamphidae* family are. These fish have a typical elongated build and occur in the wild in South-East Asia. They are typical surface fish, finding their food (mainly larvae and insects, but also dry food in the aquarium) in the top zone.

The males are recognisable by the anal fin which has been transformed into a reproductive organ, which is known as an 'andropodium' in these fish.

The best-known halfbeak is *Dermogenys pusillus*. This fish grows to a length of about 8cm and lives in small shoals. It occurs widely in Thailand, Indonesia, the Philippines and Malaysia.

Halfbeaks are often rather nervous, so they are not very well suited for keeping in a densely populated community aquarium. They will, however, live in harmony with peaceful fish which mainly occupy the middle and bottom zones. Halfbeaks are kept in small shoals. The males maintain a strict hierarchy and regularly fight to confirm the order. Since this is such a remarkable performance, these fish just like *Betta splendens* are kept in Thailand specially for fighting.

The water composition is not particularly important for halfbeaks, although they do appreciate some added salt. They are also not very demanding as regards the water temperature, and can be

Special variant of Xiphophorus helleri.

Dermogenys pusillus, *the halfbeak*

Mosquito fish

The guppy is not the only one to be entitled to the nickname of 'mosquito fish'. *Gambusia affinis holbrooki,* a small fish originating from the Southern United States and Mexico, is put out in large quantities to combat the malaria mosquito, just like its more popular neighbour. These fish are therefore not only found in their original habitats, but in other parts of the world as well, where they are thriving very well indeed.

Although scientists have been studying this species intensively for many years, it is not very well known outside scientific circles.
The black-spotted males are much smaller than the colourless females. They do not grow to

Nomorhamphus liemi liemi

Poecilia melanogaster

kept without difficulty at temperatures between 18 and 27°C.

Another halfbeak is *Nomorhamphus liemi,* a fish which is noticeable because of a strange protrusion at the end of the lower jaw in the males. This is one of the clear characteristics distinguishing the sexes, but the males also remain a few centimetres smaller than the females. Like *Dermogenys pusillus,* this halfbeak is a shoaling fish which should definitely be kept together with several others of its kind. They are only found in the southern part of the island of Celebes.

Below: Poecilia perugiae

Gambusia affinis 'holbrooki', *male*

more than 4cm in length, while the females can reach 7cm.

This species is not suitable for the average community aquarium, since the fish can sometimes adopt a rather intolerant or even aggressive attitude. The advantage of these fish is that they are very hardy and adaptable. The ideal water temperature is about 22°C, but they can also survive in temperatures of about 10°C or 35°C, provided they are not kept in these conditions for too long.

CHAPTER 5

Cichlids

Cichlids are one of the largest families of fish known to us. They come within the order of Percidae. Most species are found in Africa and Central and South America, although cichlids do occur in other parts of the world as well. It is almost impossible to describe the common characteristics of this extensive family, but one factor which all cichlids do have in common is that they care for their offspring very well and are territorial.

Variants of the angel fish (Pterophyllum scalare)

The great African lakes

Most African cichlids occur in the extensive African lakes Tanganyika, Malawi and Victoria. These lakes are vast. Lake Victoria, for example, has a water surface area of 68,000 km^2 and a depth of 80m. The well-known Lake Malawi is also huge, at 600km long. In the hard, crystal clear and mineral-rich waters of these lakes there are thousands of colourful fish varieties, the majority of which are cichlids.

Most cichlids from these lakes stand out due to their elongated shape, bright colours, and active lifestyle.

Although they live together with large numbers of their own species in the wild, they cannot always tolerate each other's company in an aquarium. The males can be particularly un-friendly. Therefore, more females than males of these cichlid species are usually kept. In most species, the sex can easily be distinguished by the noticeable differences in colour. An aquar-ium for these African cichlids almost never con-tains vegetation, but it is richly decorated with stones and pebbles. The water should be quite

Pseudotropheus zebra *is known for its aggressive character.*

Vegetation is not usually necessary in an aquarium for cichlids from the great African lakes.

Pseudotropheus lombardoi

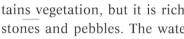

Auloloncara hansbaenschi 'Red Flash' *is a recently discovered inhabitant of Lake Malawi in Africa.*

hard, clear and rich in oxygen, and the fish appreciate bright light and plenty of movement in the water. There is usually little point in providing vegetation in the aquarium, since the fish may nibble the plants.

An aquarium which is set up specially for this type of fish will be a colourful and lively affair, which will rarely be boring. The fish are not usually difficult to feed. They will eat dry food or small live food and pieces of fish and shellfish.

Well-known cichlids from Lake Malawi

One well-known cichlid from Lake Malawi in Africa is the zebra cichlid *(Pseudotropheus zebra)*. This fish can grow to about 15cm long, and in its original form it is noticeable for its bright blue colour. Breeders have now success-

Pseudotropheus zebra, *variant*

fully bred zebra cichlids in other colours, such as the unpatterned blue and the red variants. The difference between the sexes can be seen from the whitish-yellow 'egg spots' on the male's anal fin. These egg spots have an important function. This is a mouth-brooding species: the female picks up the eggs which she has laid in her mouth immediately, even before they are fertilised by the male. In her passion to collect them all up she sees the egg spots on the male's anal fin and tries to take them into her mouth as well. At that moment the male releases his milt so that the unfertilised eggs are fertilised in her mouth. Zebra cichlids are very mobile fish. They eat both dry and live food, but they do like some vegetable food from time to time. Unfortunately this is a very aggressive species, and the males in particular can rarely tolerate each other's company.

Another Malawi cichlid which we often find in aquaria is the *Melanochromis auratus.* These colourful fish are mouth brooders like the zebra cichlid, and this is another species in which the male can be recognised by the egg spots on the anal fin. The colouring of the males is also much darker than that of the females. *Melanochromis auratus,* which is also called the nyassa cichlid, is an active fish. Unfortunately the males are very intolerant of each other. The females, on the

other hand, rarely or never fall out. Unlike many other cichlids the nyassa cichlid can be kept in an aquarium with vegetation, since this species does not dig around in the bottom or eat the plants.

Melanochromis auratus *is found in Lake Malawi in Africa.*

A group of young Melanochromis auratus

Julidochromis ornatus

The African Lamprologus occelatus *takes up residence in a snail shell.*

Cichlids from Lake Tanganyika

By far the best known cichlid which occurs in Lake Tanganyika is *Julidochromis ornatus*. The background colour of these fish is light beige and there are three dark brown horizontal stripes running along its whole body. These fish grow to about 10cm in length, although the males usually stay somewhat smaller. This *ornatus* is particularly active and, like most African cichlids, not very tolerant of others of its own kind. They occupy a territory in which they will not tolerate any other fish at all. The centre of this territory is a refuge in the form of a hollow, which is also where the eggs are laid and protected from other fish. Once the fry have hatched they are not protected or cared for any more, but the parents are not a threat to their childrens' lives. This species does not only eat dry food and small live food, but it does like some vegetable food such as algae or a blanched lettuce leaf from time to time. The *Julidochromis* genus includes many different fish, who all have the same slender build and live along the rocky shores of Lake Tanganyika. The feeding patterns and methods of reproduction for all these species are comparable with those of the *ornatus*. One very unusual occupant of Lake Tanganyika is *Lamprologus ocellatus*. These fish live on the sandy bottom of the lake and

Cichlids display interesting behaviour and are popular aquarium fish all over the world.

occupy (empty) snail shells. They are small cichlids. The males are largest but do not grow beyond 6cm. The females are a few centimetres smaller. These fish form a territory around 'their' snail shell. These fish will also need a similar shelter to be available within the aquarium.

Just like other cichlids from the African lakes, these fish feel at their best in hard, and therefore mineral-rich, water. The bottom should also consist of well-washed sand, not gravel. One difficult aspect about keeping these fish is that they seldom accept dry food.

Other Africans

Apart from the many varieties of cichlids from the great African lakes, there are many other species of cichlids found in Africa. One of these has been a popular aquarium fish for decades: the purple cichlid, which has the scientific name *Pelvicachromis pulcher*. These cichlids and

Male purple cichlids are larger than females and also do not have the purplish-red stomach to which this species owes its name.

their close relations live along the overgrown banks of rivers near the west coast of Africa. The water in which they live is very different from the water in the great African lakes. It is moderately hard and slightly acidic. In some of their habitats the water has a fairly high salt content.

The purple cichlid can be kept in a community aquarium with plenty of vegetation and refuges, and will adjust very well to water whose composition is different from its own natural biotope. These fish grow to no more than 8cm long and are not particularly aggressive. They do protect their territory, which is usually situated around their refuge close to the bottom. The behaviour of these fish is particularly interesting. If a pair of purple cichlids are well looked after, it will not be long before they start a family. Both parents care for and protect their eggs and fry. They are not very demanding as regards their food. They

Apistogramma agassizi comes from the Amazon region of South America.

Nannochromis transvestitus *comes from West Africa. This is a female.*

Nannochromis transvestitus, *male*

will normally readily accept dry food, but they also like regular live food, such as mosquito larvae, tubifex and water fleas.

The brightly coloured and aggressive Red Acara *(Hemichromis bimaculatus)* is also a well-known aquarium fish from Africa. This species can grow to about 12cm long and will, like the purple cichlid, reproduce readily in an aquar-ium. Unlike the purple cichlid, however, these fish have the disadvantage of being very intolerant or even downright aggressive towards their neighbours. Due to this characteristic, they are not well suited for the community aquarium. They are usually kept in larger aquaria together with a number of other robust cichlid species.

However the way in which these fish treat their eggs and young is touching to behold. The fry are jealously defended by both parents against curious and hungry neighbours.

Large cichlids from South and Central America

Many cichlids which are found in South and Central America are giants among tropical aquarium fish. Most of them can grow to 20cm or even longer. It is impossible to deny that these fish have some degree of intelligence. They have an expressive appearance, and their mood can be easily recognised from the ever-changing colours, the position of their fins and their whole expression. It is partly for this reason that these South Americans have become very popular aquarium fish. Cichlids from this region are found in large rivers such as the Rio Negro, Orinoco and Amazon and their tributaries. They mainly live along the banks, amidst dense vegetation, and eat shrimps, fish and insect larvae.

The angel fish *(Pterophyllum Scalare)* is probably the best known and most popular South

A small African cichlid, Pelvicachromis suboccelatus, *female*

Discus fish are splendid but very sensitive fish which can grow to about 20cm long.

Previous pages: Symphysodon aequifasciatus 'Royal Blue'

American cichlid. Angel fish are quiet, peaceful fish whose height exceeds their length. In order to provide enough room for these fish the aquarium must be quite high. These fish need peace and quiet and it is better not to keep them together with predatory fish, but keeping them in company with very small fish is not recommended either. The original colour of the angel fish is beige with black transverse bands and red colouring around the eyes, but a huge number of variants have now been bred. We now have white, golden, pure black, marbled and spotted angel fish, and there is also a long-finned form which is very much in vogue.

Angel fish must always be kept in a shoal. They enjoy each other's company and even the males get on well together. Since they are not very sensitive to the water composition, they make a good choice for beginners. Too much current in the water does not help the fish to stay in a good mood. In the wild they often seek shelter in overgrown riverbanks.

One fish which looks very similar to the angel fish and is sometimes confused with it by lay people is the *Pterophyllum altum*. The external difference between these fish is that the *Pte-*

rophyllum altum, when seen from the side, has a dent above its mouth, while the head of the angel fish runs almost straight or in a slight curve into its dorsal fin. There is not much demand for these fish, because they make stringent demands on the water composition and are very sensitive.

Cichlasoma meeki, better known as the firemouth cichlid, grows to about 15cm in length. These robust fish originate from Central and South America. They are found particularly frequently on the Yucatan peninsula. During the mating season the males can be recognised by their bright red stomach and throat area. Firemouth cichlids are territorial cichlids, but they have a moderate temperament and are not aggressive. The firemouth cichlid likes to dig around, so an aquarium has to be specially set up for these fish. A thick layer of gravel, which should not be too coarse, gives the fish plenty of opportunity to display its natural behaviour. A firemouth cichlid will not leave plant roots alone, so it is better only to use very hardy plants in this type of aquarium, protecting their roots by means of a buried flowerpot.

One popular, but also sensitive and vulnerable, South American is the discus fish. There are two

Right: Breeding pair of Pterophyllum scalare

Discus fish, variant

original types of this disc-shaped cichlid, the *Symphysodon aequifasciata* and the *Symphysodon discus*. The latter variant has a rather shorter body.

Since these fish occur in various different guises in nature and the two variants cross-breed, it is not always easy to distinguish them from each other. Discus fish are always kept in a special aquarium, usually without the company of other species. They like acidic, soft water, and the temperature must never fall below 26°C, because if it does they will fall ill. Since it is so difficult to keep these fish healthy, they are quite expensive to buy and are almost exclusively kept by advanced aquarists. Discus fish are rather nervous and will not simply accept all the food they are given. These fish are also quite fussy about their choice of a partner, but a pair will sometimes form from a large shoal which can get along.

Breeding pair of Pterrophyllum scalare

Discus fish are excellent parents. The fry eat a discharge from the parents' mucous membranes at first, and then they go off to look for food for themselves.

Cichlasoma nigrofasciatum

The male firemouth cichlid *mainly lives up to his name during the mating season.*

Astrontus ocellatus, better known as the oscar cichlid, is one of the fastest-growing cichlids. It is a real glutton, and has to be fed several times a day. These large fish will quickly devour dry food, all kinds of live food and pieces of meat, fish and shellfish. When the fish are young they have an attractive dark background with a remarkable orange or red pattern on their flanks which is never the same on any two fish. Once they are mature the colours fade to a bronze-yellow. What does remain is the typical round spot just in front of the tail fin, which the fish is named after in some languages.

Oscar cichlids can grow to 30cm long (or longer) and are reasonably active, certainly at feeding time. They get on well together. They are not aggressive, but it is better not to keep them together with smaller species. The aquarium needs to be very large. A powerful motorised filter to keep the water clean and in motion will definitely be needed. The water composition is not particularly important for this species, as long as the water is clear and pure.

Melanochromis 'Cherokee'

Symphysodon aequifasciatus 'Royal Blue'

Small American cichlids

Most small American cichlids are suitable for keeping in a medium-sized community aquarium. These are usually quite peaceful and tolerant fish, so they can live together in harmony even with smaller (shoaling) fish. One of the best species is *Microgeophagus Ramirezi*, which used to be known as *Apistogramma Ramirezi*. This is known in English as the butterfly cichlid. These colourful fish are found in still and slow-moving waters in Colombia and Venezuela. They do not grow to more than 6cm in length, and are usually smaller than that. Their bright colouring and unusual behaviour makes them an attractive species to keep. They like water which is soft and slightly acidic. They usually remain in the bottom zone and do not rush about very much.

Butterfly cichlids are always kept as a pair. The difference between the sexes can be seen from the foremost fin rays on the dorsal fin. These are longer and also darker in colour in the male than in the female.

Once they have found their favourite place in the aquarium they will stay close to it all the time. This territory will be defended, but not as fanatically as many other cichlids do. These fish usually lay their eggs on a flat piece of stone and

Microgeophagus ramirezi, *the butterfly cichlid*

look after both their eggs and their fry very carefully.

In addition to the butterfly cichlid we also know a number of small American cichlids which are often kept as aquarium fish.
Apistogramma agassizi is one of these. Just like its family members *Apistogramma borelli* and *Apistogramma cacatuoides*, these cichlids do not grow to more than 8cm in lenght. The females stay even smaller than this, and are usually only 4 to 5 cm long. These cichlids have adjusted well to life in an aquarium. They do very well in soft to moderately hard water, but they are sensitive to pollution. It will therefore be necessary to refresh part of the aquarium water at least once a week. Refuges such as dense vegetation, bogwood and stones are well used by these territorial fish. Fish of this species like small live food and sometimes refuse to eat dry food.

Papiliochromis altispinosus

Establishing a territory is a characteristic of all cichlids.

Lamprologus *spec.* 'Daffodil'

CHAPTER 6

Carps

Carps and members of the carp family are found almost throughout the world, with the exception of Australia and South America. Most carp varieties like to live in a shoal, but there are also some types of carp which are definitely solitary.

Barbus tetrazona, *the sumatran*

Sub-family Cyprininae

The *Cyprininae* sub-family belongs to the large family of *Cyprinidae* or carps, together with the sub-families *Rasborinae* and *Garrinae*. The sub-family *Cyprininae* includes a large number of popular aquarium fish. The goldfish (*Carassius auratus*) is one of these, and the koi carp also belongs to the same sub-family.

The goldfish does not really need any introduction. This species is the most popular aquarium fish in the world, but unfortunately it is all too often not kept correctly. The well-known goldfish bowl is by no means a suitable type of accommodation for this colourful fish. An ideal goldfish aquarium should be large, with crystal-clear water rich in oxygen.

Goldfish do not like to be alone, and should always be kept together with a few others of its

Calico veiltail goldfish

kind. They like to dig in the bottom, so this should consist of fine, rounded gravel. Goldfish are easy to feed, but besides dry food they also need some live food and vegetable food. In the absence of vegetable food the goldfish will nibble at the leaves of plants. Goldfish can grow very large. The species with normal build can

Red Cap veiltail goldfish

exceed 20cm in length, depending on the swimming space available to them. The fantails and other variants are usually rather smaller.

Cyprininae – *the genus* Barbus

Barbs are tough and powerful shoaling fish from Asia. The barb genus includes a number of popular aquarium fish, for example *Barbus tetrazona,* which is better known as the Sumatran. Many colour variants of these Indonesian shoaling fish have now been bred, but the original form is still the most popular. Sumatrans are strong, lively fish which are very well suited to the community aquarium, as long as their company does not include fish with long fins or feelers.

This is because Sumatrans have an irresistible tendency to nibble at these. Sumatrans grow to about 6cm long, and can be kept in a medium-sized or large aquarium. They are not difficult to feed. Sumatrans eat both dry food and small live food, but they do like vegetable food from time to time.

Barbus conchonius (the rosy barb) is one of the most robust barbs. These fish are therefore rightly recommended for beginners. Rosy barbs are lively, good-natured fish. They do not need as much warmth as other barbs, and can be kept perfectly well in unheated aquaria in the living room, and in the garden pond during the summer.

The difference between the sexes is very easy to see from their body colour: males have much more red pigment than females. Specialised centres usually offer normal rosy barbs, but there is also a long-finned variant which is no less robust than the original. Rosy barbs grow to about 7cm in length in the aquarium, but if they have more space available, they can certainly reach twice that length.

Barbus titteya, the sherry barb, is found in Sri Lanka. Due to their small size and moderate activity these little barbs are perfect for keeping

Koi carp have been very popular for centuries.

The moss-green sumatran is a specially bred variant.

Following pages: Barbus titteya *is also known as the sherry barb.*

in a smaller aquarium. They can be rather shy if the aquarium does not provide enough refuge, and very bright lighting will not help them to feel at ease either.

If they are kept correctly, in an aquarium with dense vegetation, plenty of floating vegetation and quiet neighbours, the males will display a splendid red colour – particularly during the mating season. Sherry barbs enjoy the company of others of their kind, but they can also be kept as a pair.

The rosy barb is a suitable fish for beginners.

Sub-family Rasborinae

The sub-family *Rasborinae* includes a small, popular shoaling fish from Southern China, the Chinese danio. The scientific name of this fish, *Tanichthys albonubes*, refers to its place of origin and the boy who first discovered the fish. According to the story, a number of these fish were found in the 1930s by a small Chinese boy named Tan. He is said to have caught his danios in a stream in the White Cloud Mountains.

The Chinese danio is a small and slender shoaling fish which, like the rosy barb, can easily be kept in an unheated aquarium. They are lively, friendly and active fish which swim throughout the middle and top zones. They grow to about 4cm long and do not need very much space.

It is, however, necessary to keep them in a shoal. The difference between the sexes can be seen not only from the female's fatter stomach, but also from their colour. This is because the males have more intense colouring than the females.

Golden danio

The sub-family *Rasborinae* includes two genera which in turn account for a large number of popular aquarium fish. Well-known species within the *Brachydanio* genus include the zebra danio *(Brachydanio rerio)* and the golden danio *(Brachydanio albinoleatus)*.

The zebra danio grows to a maximum length of 5cm. It is a very active swimmer which must definitely be kept in a shoal. The aquarium does not have to be very large, but it must have a cover, since the antics of these fish include regularly jumping up out of the water. This small species from India is known for its peaceable nature and also for its toughness. They are the perfect fish for those starting out with aquarium fish. When it comes to feeding they are easy to satisfy, and enjoy both dry food and small live food. Zebra danios are free layers, which means that they expel their eggs and then pay no more attention to them. A long-finned variety of the zebra danio has now been bred, and there is also a spotted variant which is known as *Brachydanio frankei*, the leopard danio.

The golden danio, like its smaller family member, is a fast-swimming shoaling fish which will do well in various water types and is quite easy to look after. These fish need plenty of open space for swimming and are rarely seen near vegetation. This fish originally comes from Asia, but it will easily reproduce in the aquarium.

The Chinese danio can be kept in unheated aquaria.

Golden danios are free layers. If a good breeding pair is transferred to a separate breeding tank in which the temperature is a few degrees higher than what the fish are used to, they will soon lay their eggs. After laying both parents must be caught immediately, as otherwise they will see their own eggs as a welcome addition to their diet.

The genus Rasbora

All fish of the genus *Rasbora* come from South-East Asia, mainly from countries like Thailand, Indonesia and Malaysia. The smallest fish in this genus is *Rasbora maculata*. These shoaling fish do not grow beyond 2.5cm in length. They like peace and quiet and lead a sheltered life amongst dense vegetation.

They are suitable for keeping in a community aquarium, as long as there are enough refuges and the neighbours are not too rough or intolerant.

The zebra danio is a shoaling fish from India.

Rasbora maculata

Rasbora heteromorpha *was one of the first tropical fish to be kept in Europe.*

Rasbora heteromorpha, or the harlequin fish, arrived in Europe at the beginning of this century, and very quickly became one of the most sought after aquarium fish of all. The natural biotope of the harlequin fish is the Asian jungle, where they live in shallow pools amongst the foliage, chasing small insects and their larvae. They are not demanding fish, and they have adapted excellently to life in the aquarium. They

are quite robust and can grow to a considerable age, as long as the aquarium water is soft and slightly acidic. They like to live in a shoal and are fairly active. They sometimes squabble amongst themselves, but leave other fish alone.

Sub-family Garrinae

Epalzeorhynchus bicolor, better known as the red-finned black shark or under its former scientific name *Labeo bicolor,* is a remarkable fish.

It is the best-known aquarium fish within the *Garrinae* sub-family, with a velvety black body and a bright red tail. Red-finned black sharks are definitely solitary creatures. If more than one adult are kept in the same aquarium it is very likely that they will fight almost continuously.

Epalzeorhynchus frenatus

Red-finned black shark (Epalzeorhynchus bicolor)

Older red-finned black sharks are not usually very friendly towards other fish, but this malevolent characteristic has not adversely affected the popularity of this remarkable aquarium fish.

An aquarium for a red-finned black shark must provide sufficient space for this fish, which can grow to 20cm long, and there must also be adequate refuges.

These fish form a territory near to pieces of bogwood and dense vegetation. The difference between males and females is virtually impossible to distinguish. A trained eye will only be

able to spot the more heavily built female when the fish are fully grown and mature.

The *Epalzeorhynchus frenatus* has the same characteristics as the red-finned black shark, and when young the two may be confused. As they

Barbus pentazona pentazona

Barbus ticto

grow older the *frenatus* turns out to be a paler colour, which makes it less popular as an aquarium fish.

Family Cobitidae

The *Cobitidae* (loach) family is a member of the carp group. This family has a number of typical characteristics. Many of these fishes can not only use their gills for respiration, but they can also absorb oxygen through their intestines. This allows them to survive in the deoxygenated water in which these species of fish are often found in the wild. Their mouth is downward-facing and they have a flat stomach, which indicates that they are bottom dwellers. Many members of this family have wicked-looking spines near their eyes, which they can use to defend themselves when necessary.

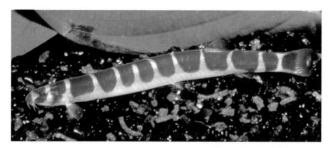

Pangio kuhlii *can be kept either as a solitary fish or with others of its kind.*

Clown loach

Botia lohachata

The species which has the most obvious spines is *Pangio kuhlii,* the Indian loach. These mobile and peaceful 'little snakes' are found in the tropical forests of South-East Asia. They hide during the day, and become active during the evening. Indian loaches mainly eat small worms and insect larvae, and think nothing of delving deep into the (soft) bottom to find them. They are curious and interesting fish to keep, and are well suited to life in a community aquarium. In the wild they are usually solitary, but in the aquarium it has been found that they get on together very well.

In order to keep these fish correctly the substrate in the aquarium needs to be soft. Refuges in the form of root wood in convoluted shapes, combined with dense vegetation, will also be attractive to an Indian loach. In their natural biotope the water is very acidic and soft because of the many dead and rotting leaves and branches which end up in the shallow streams and pools.
In the aquarium these fish will nevertheless do quite well in different water types.

The clown loach *(Botia macracantha),* which also originates from South-East Asia, is really a social fish. If this fish is kept in isolation it will eventually begin to interfere with the other inhabitants of the aquarium. Keeping them as a pair is not recommended either, since the stronger of the two will constantly chase the weaker, and will sometimes become so aggressive that the weaker fish cannot survive. In a shoal of five or six, however, problems rarely arise. The fish will form a lively and colourful whole, and will often engage in mock fights which do not cause much harm.

The clown loach is a popular aquarium fish due to its splendid colouring and comical appearance, but unfortunately this species is rather susceptible to disease. In order to prevent the fish falling sick it is necessary to keep the water temperature at at least 25°C, and the acidity of the water must also be enhanced by using peat. Clown loaches can grow to about 15cm in the aquarium, depending on the swimming space available.

Rasbora pauciperforata

Another loach is *Botia lohachata*. This species is built very much like the clown loach, but it is much smaller. Its behaviour is also very different from that of its more popular family member. This loach does not become active until dusk and night-time, while the clown loach is on the go virtually all day long.

Botia lohachata is also not a fish which enjoys life in a shoal or in the open water. It prefers its own company and will look for shelter.

Epalzeorhynchus kallopterus

CHAPTER 7

Labyrinth fish

For many species of fish the water composition is vitally important. If pollution or climate changes alter their living environment, they cannot survive. Occasionally, however, we find fish which have learned to adapt to extreme circumstances. Labyrinth fish, which are also known under the scientific name *Belontidae*, are a good example of this.

The labyrinth allows labyrinth fish to absorb oxygen directly from the atmosphere.

Colisa lalia, *variant*

The labyrinth

Labyrinth fish belong to a very popular group of aquarium fish. They owe their name to an organ which is situated at the back of the head in these fish, the so-called 'labyrinth'. This labyrinth allows the fish not only to take in oxygen from the water through their gills, but also to take it directly from the atmosphere. This allows these fish to survive in water which contains little or

The water in which labyrinth fish live can be very shallow and sometimes contains large quantities of waste and little oxygen.

no oxygen. In the aquarium, whether or not it contains sufficient oxygen, labyrinth fish must have an opportunity to come up to the surface for air. If they cannot, there is a good chance that they will suffocate, because respiration through their gills usually does not produce enough oxygen. Labyrinth fish can become sick if the difference between the water temperature and the atmospheric temperature is too great. A cover is therefore always placed on the aquarium for these fish.

A hard existence

The vast majority of labyrinth fish are found in South-East Asia. They are found in shallow rice fields and small puddles, ponds and pools.

The conditions in which labyrinth fish are kept in the aquarium are much better than in the wild.

Colisa lalia comes from India.

In this environment periods of drought are alternated with heavy rainfall. When the rain comes, the fish have few difficulties. Large areas of land are flooded and the fish can therefore swim to wherever the conditions are most favourable. There is plenty of live food and the water is fairly clear and rich in oxygen.

It is not until continuing drought causes the water level to fall fast that most fish get into difficulties. Escape routes are cut off by the steady fall in the water level. The large area of water is slowly but surely reduced to hundreds of small pools and ponds, sometimes no deeper than five or ten centimetres. Thousands of fish are forced to pack into these puddles. Due to the large number of fish and their excrement the stagnant water becomes polluted very quickly

and the available oxygen is soon used up. Waste materials accumulate and the blazing sunshine raises the temperature to well over 30°C. This causes the fish to become breathless. Normal fish, which are dependent on their gills for respiration, simply die.

Labyrinth fish, however, have their labyrinth, which allows them to take oxygen directly from the atmosphere just like people. There is usually no shortage of food. Mosquitos and many other insects lay their eggs on the surface of the water, and both the insects themselves and their eggs and larvae are devoured by the labyrinth fish. This allows them to live for a long time, until a good shower of rain links the puddles together again and the fish can once again swim away to a better place.

Verzorging

Most labyrinth fish are quiet creatures with a ponderous manner. They usually populate the top zone, where they search for insect larvae on the water surface.

They are not particularly good swimmers, and they can therefore be well accommodated in smaller aquaria. They definitely appreciate peace and quiet.

If they are kept in an aquarium with strong, aggressive species, they will definitely not feel at home. Their colours fade and they retreat to a quiet spot. It is therefore better only to keep

Left: small shoaling fish like this Rasbora maculata *are perfect company for smaller labyrinth fish.*

Below: Corydoras sterbai. *These little fish can be kept in almost any aquarium and tend to keep to themselves.*

these fish together with quiet shoaling fish which occupy the middle zone, and bottom dwellers will also do very well in this type of aquarium.

An aquarium housing labyrinth fish should not be excessively aerated. This causes a strong flow in the water, which these fish do not like. Given the conditions in which they live in their

Betta splendens -- *males are very aggressive towards each other.*

natural habitats, this is not surprising. They do like dense soft-leafed vegetation on the water surface, which allows them to move slowly and ponderously through the leaves. With a few exceptions, most fish in this family do not like low water temperatures.

The female Betta imbellis *looks very similar to* Betta splendens.

These fish need warmth and water temperatures between 25°C and 28°C on average are ideal. Labyrinth fish are not difficult in terms of feeding. Most of them have no difficulty eating dry food, but they do like some small live food, such as mosquito larvae, brine shrimps and water fleas. They will also take wingless fruit flies.

The kissing gourami is one exception, which does like some live food but mainly eats algae and other vegetable food.

Social characteristics

Most labyrinth fish are best kept as a pair, or with a single male combined with two or three females. The males are very active lovers and their constant chasing does nothing for the females' peace of mind. In a small aquarium without many refuges for the female, chasing by

Labyrinth fish are easy to feed.

the males quickly leads to problems, particularly if the female is not planning to give in to his advances.

Males do not always get on very well together, either, although this certainly does not apply to all labyrinth fish. One notorious species is *Betta splendens,* which is better known as the Siamese fighting fish. More than one male of this species can never be kept in the aquarium, since two males will fight until one of them is dead.

However they are very friendly towards their neighbours. The more aggressive labyrinth fish may see small fish in the aquarium as live food, but most of the fish in this family are very peaceful.

Colisa lalia, *variant*

Reproduction

Reproduction among labyrinth fish is very interesting. Most of the brood care is done by the male.

He uses small air bubbles to build a nest of foam on the water surface, sometimes supported by small pieces of vegetation. He then courts the female in a dazzling mating ritual and while the eggs and milt are being expelled the pair writhe around each other to increase the likelihood of fertilisation.

After mating the females are no longer tolerated near the nest. In the wild the females can escape, but in the aquarium there is nowhere to go. In order to protect the females against the male's aggression, they are netted out after mating.

The male will then take the eggs, which have sunk to the bottom, in his mouth one by one and take them to the nest, where he carefully places each one.

Until they hatch the male will continue to guard his offspring. Intruders and curious fish will be steadfastly chased away by the male. Once the fry begin to swim the protective instinct disappears and the male begins to see his offspring with different eyes. This is the time to transfer the male to a different aquarium as well.

Sub-family Trichogasterinae

This sub-family includes a number of very popular aquarium fish. *Colisa lalia*, which comes from India, is one of these. This is a brightly coloured and peaceful fish which can grow to about 6cm long. It is very suitable for breeding in aquaria, and various colours have now been produced.

The original type, the male of which is bright

blue with red stripes, is still the most popular. The colouring of the female is much more boring. The sexes can therefore easily be distinguished. Like virtually all labyrinth fish they are not very sensitive to the water composition, which makes them very well suited to beginners. Another small labyrinth fish which comes from India is *Colisa sota*, which used to be known by the

Trichogaster leeri

Below: Colisa fasciata *(photograph)* and Colisa labiosa *look very similar.*

The original form of Colisa lalia *is so far still the most popular.*

scientific name of *Colisa chuna*. This fish grows to only 4.5cm long. It is quite a shy and retiring fish which will be forced into the vegetation by more aggressive species. The male will not show his splendid deep copper body colour and pitch black chest until the fish feel completely comfortable.

This sub-family has certain larger and more robust members such as *Trichogaster leeri* and *Trichogaster trichopteris*, which are known as the pearl gourami and blue gourami. These fish grow quite large and therefore belong in large aquaria with plenty of space for swimming. They appreciate dense feathery-leafed peripheral vegetation.

In the wild they are found in Indonesia, Malaysia and Thailand. These are also predominantly quiet fish. They leave even the smallest aquarium dwellers in peace.

Trichogaster trichopterus

The pearl gourami does not have any coloured variants, but the blue gourami is now available in

Trichogaster trichopterus, *special variant*

Chocolate gouramis are particularly attractive fish, but they are difficult to keep in good condition.

Colisa sota is a shy but peaceful and interesting fish.

many different colours, such as marbled blue and marbled yellow.

Colisa labiosa and *Colisa fasciata* look very similar, and they are therefore quite often confused. *Colisa fasciata* is the largest of the two, and can grow to more than 10cm long. *Colisa labiosa* will be a few centimetres smaller than this. Both species are suitable for the community aquarium and are not very sensitive to water composition.

Finally, the chocolate gourami, with the complicated scientific name *Sphaerichthys osphromenoides*, is the most difficult of these species to keep in good condition. These fish, which come from Indonesia, are very demanding indeed as

regards the aquarium water. The water should definitely be soft and also rather acidic if the fish are to feel comfortable. In other water types they will quickly become sick. These peaceful fish grow to about 5cm long and are quite shy.

Sub-family Macropodinae

The sub-family *Macropodinae* includes two very well-known and popular aquarium fish: *Betta splendens*, or the Siamese fighting fish, and *Macropodus opercularis*, the paradise fish. The paradise fish was the first sub-tropical fish to be kept in Europe. They became very popular at the time, due to their great adaptability and the fact that these fish are very well able to withstand temperature fluctuations and can be kept in unheated water.

They are not so widely seen these days. Nevertheless these fish, whose original habitats are in China, Taiwan and Korea, are definitely worth keeping. The males are very intolerant towards each other and small fish in the aquarium will be seen as tasty morsels. The male paradise fish can grow to about 10cm long, but the females are smaller.

Betta splendens, the Siamese fighting fish

Macropodus opercularis, *the paradise fish, can be kept in an unheated home aquarium.*

A male Siamese fighting fish with aquamarine colouring

There is no labyrinth fish with such obvious differences between the sexes as the Siamese fighting fish. The females are small and unremarkable, while the larger males are an amazing sight with their tremendously long fins and spectacular range of colours. Siamese fighting fish come in various colours, although the red, blue and aquamarine coloured fish are most popular.

Betta splendens, with its huge fins, is a variant of the original form which is much more modest in appearance.

The males are very aggressive towards each other. It is impossible to keep two males even in large aquaria, because they will definitely find each other and fight. These fights are so violent and serious that they usually result in the death of one of the fish. In Thailand the fights between male Siamese fighting fish are extremely popular and they are also regularly organised. This species does very well in a community aquarium, as long as there are no fish which are too small. If they are left alone Siamese fighting fish will keep to themselves. They are quite robust, but are not very good at coping with water temperatures of below 24°C.

Helostomatidae

There is only one species in this family, and that is the kissing gourami or *Helostoma temminckii*. This fish is specially bred for its meat in the regions where it comes from. The kissing gourami owes its name to the typical behaviour displayed by rival males. They grip each other by the mouth and continue to pull at each other's mouth until the weaker one gives up. For a long time it was thought that this behaviour was related to the courtship ritual, but since it is virtually only males which display this behaviour, the theory was later overturned. Kissing gouramis can grow very large. In their natural habitats, Thailand and some of the islands of Indonesia, they grow to more than 30cm long, but in the aquarium most of them do not even reach half that size.

A blue Siamese fighting fish

Kissing gouramis are eaten in their country of origin, but elsewhere they enjoy their status as popular and useful aquarium fish. This is the pink variant. The wild form is grey-green in colour and less popular with aquarists.

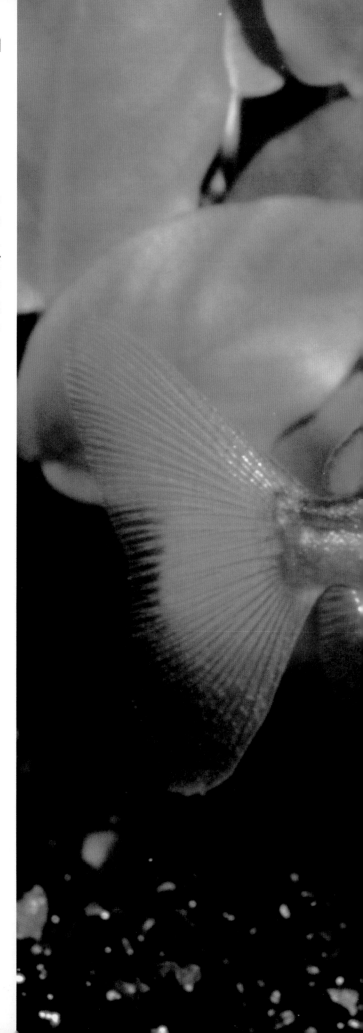

CHAPTER 8

Salmonoids

The huge group of salmonoids includes many well-known aquarium fish. These originally come from Africa and South America, mainly along the banks of shallow rivers. Most salmonoids are relatively small, peace-loving shoaling fish, but the feared piranha also belongs to this group.

Metynnis maculatus

Shoaling fish

Most characins are shoaling fish, which means that they always swim close together. Many shoaling fish are an easy target for predators. They are small and nature has not given them any means of defence. The fish therefore have no option but to carry on swimming close together, tightly packed together. Some predators see such a group as one large fish, a fish which is larger than the predator itself, and therefore leaves them alone.

The shoal is the power of all shoaling fish, so they are very social. Even the males hardly ever cause any problems. Many shoaling fish mate within the shoal for safety reasons and therefore do not separate from the group. In order to warn each other when there is a threat of danger, these fish give off a kind of warning substance which is immediately picked up by the others and gives the fish a chance to flee quickly.

Solitary shoaling fish never feel entirely comfortable. They spend their time nervously looking for others of their kind, and their colours fade. They also feel insecure in shoals which are too small and quickly take fright even when there is no danger looming at all. These fish should therefore always be kept in a shoal. The recommended minimum is always five, but it goes without saying that it is better to keep a much larger shoal than that. Moreover, a large shoal such as this gives a much more attractive overall effect.

Characins (Characidae)

The characin family is a large one, of which the sub-family *Tetragonopterinae* includes the best-known and most popular aquarium fish. Characins are peace-loving, relatively small shoaling fish which are sometimes found in shoals of thousands in the wild. They occur in South and Central America. This large sub-family is subdivided into a number of genera.

The genus *Paracheirodon*

The cardinal tetra *(Paracheirodon axelrodi)* and the neon tetra *(Paracheirodon innesi)* belong to the genus *Paracheirodon*. These are small fish. The cardinal tetra grows to about 5cm long, while the neon tetra is usually a centimetre smaller than that. Their spectacular neon colours are not actually seen at their best when the fish are kept in large shoals, for example with

Hyphessobrycon robertsi

Paracheirodon axelrodi, *the cardinal tetra, is found in the wild in shoals containing thousands.*

Neon tetra, variant

twenty or thirty together. These fish occupy the middle zone and they are fairly active. The neon tetra is particularly well liked because this species is not only cheaper to buy but also rather more robust than the cardinal tetra. No variants are (yet) known of the cardinal tetra, but the neon tetra is now also sold as a long-finned variant.

These are very peaceful fish. They can be kept in smaller or larger aquariums. They will readily accept both dry food and small live food, and if they are well cared for both species can grow to quite an old age.

The genus *Hyphessobrycon*

The genus *Hyphessobrycon* includes innumerable different fish, many of which are very similar. Well known ones include *Hyphessobrycon bentosi* and *Hyphessobrycon flammeus*, the red rio. Both are definitely shoaling fish and are quite small, rarely exceeding 4cm in length. Since they are very strong and can also live in less than ideal water conditions, these variants

Hyphessobrycon flammeus, the red rio, is one of the most robust aquarium fish of all.

Hyphessobrycon bentosi rosaceus

are popular with beginners. They like a small amount of movement in the water and dense peripheral vegetation with feathery-leafed plants. In brightly lit aquaria with a light substrate they will hardly display any colour at all, but if a shadowy background is created these fish will show their splendid shades of red. They are easy fish to feed, and although they will certainly appreciate live food, they can remain perfectly healthy on a menu of exclusively high-quality dry food.

Other well-known aquarium fish in this genus are the lemon tetra *(Hyphessobrycon pulchri-*

Hyphessobrycon pulchripinnis

pinnis) and the black neon *(Hyphessobrycon herbertaxelrodi)*, both of which are small, friendly shoaling fish which will quickly make

Hyphessobrycon herbertaxelrodi

Hemigrammus caudovittatus

themselves at home in a shady aquarium with soft, rather acidic water.

The genus *Hemigrammus*

The glowlight tetra is a fish which looks very much like the cardinal tetra and the neon tetra. However it is still (so far) classified with the genus *Hemigrammus,* which also includes the Buenos Aires tetra *(Hemigrammus caudivittatus).* The glowlight tetra is a small shoaling fish with a sparkling bright orange luminous strip along its almost colourless body. These fish and their markings only really come into their own against a dark background and in subdued lighting. The difference between the sexes can be seen from the size and shape of the stomach. The females have a fatter stomach, whose shape is also rounder. Glowlight tetras are usually active, peaceful fish which keep rather to themselves and leave the other inhabitants of the aquarium alone.

The Buenos Aires tetra used to be one of the

Paracheirodon erythrozonus

most popular aquarium fish of all, at a time when technology was not as advanced as it is now. These shoaling fish, which come from South America can very easily be kept in unheated aquaria in a living room, as long as the temperature does not fall below 17°C. Their colours do, however, show up better if the aquarium water is

The iridescent points on the body of Moenkhausia pittieri are at their best against a dark substrate in a moderately lit aquarium.

Below: Moenkhausia sanctaefilomenae

kept at a temperature of about 24°C. These tough fish can be kept easily in virtually all water types. Buenos Aires tetras are lively and definitely have to be kept in a shoal. The great disadvantage associated with keeping these fish, and which has meant that the fish are no longer quite so popular, is that they like to nibble at soft-leaved plants. They are therefore usually kept in aquaria with no plants or with very robust, tough-leafed plant varieties.

The genus *Moenkhausia*

There are two popular aquarium fish belonging to the genus *Moenkhausia*. The diamond tetra *(Moenkhausia pittieri)* is one of these. This is a reasonably active shoaling fish. Diamond tetra are always kept in a shoal. The difference between the males and females can be seen at a glance in full-grown fish. Not only are the males larger, but their fins are also much longer than those of the females.

Like all fish in this sub-family, diamond tetra are also free layers, which means that they expel their eggs and then do not take care of them. Moreover, the eggs are sometimes seen as an addition to their menu.

The breeding tank is therefore always fitted with a substrate spawner which is fitted a few centi-metres above the bottom. The eggs fall through the grill, so that the parents can no longer reach them.

The genus *Nematobrycon*

The best-known fish in this genus is the emperor tetra *(Nematobrycon palmeri)*, which comes from Colombia. This attractive fish grows to about 6cm in length and, like all other chara-cins, lives in shoals.

These fish with their typical, easily recognisable body shape are not particularly active and occupy the lower and middle zones. The difference between males and females of this species is easy to see in adults; the males are not only larger than the females, but their dorsal and tail fins are longer. The emperor tetra is rather sensitive

Nematobrycon lacortei

Nematobrycon palmeri, *the emperor tetra*

One fish which closely resembles the emperor tetra is *Nematobrycon lacortei*. The most obvious differences between these two species are limited to the area around the eyes, which is red in *Nematobrycon lacortei* and bluish-green in the emperor tetra. The body of *Nematobrycon lacortei* is also a lighter golden colour.

Other American characins

Other characins originating from South and Central America and belonging to the sub-family *Tetragonopterinae* are, for example, *Megalamprologus megalopterus* and *Megalamprologus sweglesi*, better known by the popular names of black phantom tetra and red phantom tetra. These are fairly quiet shoaling fish which do very well in a community aquarium. The females of these two species are noticeable in that they are more colourful than the males,

to the water composition, and should ideally be kept in rather acidic and soft water at a temperature of about 26°C.

Megalamprologus megalopterus

and this is fairly unique in the fish world, where it is usually the males which are better endowed in this area. The males do, however, have a larger dorsal fin.

Even more remarkable is *Astyanax Mexicanus* or the blind cave tetra. This Mexican species still has eyes when it is young, but as it grows older they gradually disappear. These fish are found in water in caves, and seem not to be troubled by their handicap at all. Blind cave tetras grow to

Hasemania nana, *the silver tipped tetra*

Astyanax mexicanus, *the blind cave tetra, still has (small) eyes when young, but it loses them later on.*

about 8cm long and the females can be recognised by their fuller stomach. These fish do very well in a community aquarium and usually occupy the middle zone. Blind cave tetras are robust and can adapt to various different types of water composition. Water at a temperature of about 22°C is ideal.

Another well-known aquarium fish is *Hasemania nana*. This is a small, peace-loving shoaling fish with a copper-coloured body and white tips on its fins. The colour of these fish shows up particularly well in an aquarium with a dark substrate and plenty of floating vegetation. They like soft, acidic and well-oxygenated water with some flow.

Hatchet fish (Gasteropelecidae)

Hatchet fish are found in the northern part of South America. There are many different types of hatchet fish, but they all have the same typical body shape. The most noticeable differences are restricted to their colours, patterns and size. The smallest of all is *Carnegiella myersi*, a fish only 2.5cm long, and the largest species can grow to

Carnegiella strigata strigata

Hatchet fish like this *Thoracocharax securis* can leap high out of the water.

Below: Nannostomus trifasciatus

about 9cm. Hatchet fish are shoaling fish. They prefer to live just under the surface of the water. In the wild their food consists of insects and their larvae, but in the aquarium they are just as happy to eat dry food. Sometimes they jump up out of the water to grab an insect, and partly due to their high pectoral fins they can fly along the surface of the water. A lid on the aquarium that closes properly is therefore not an unnecessary luxury. Hatchet fish are fairly peaceful, and live other aquarium dwellers alone.

The Lebiasinidae *family*

The *Lebiasinidae* family consists of two sub-families, of which *Pyrrhulininae* is the only one which is important for aquarists. This includes the genera *Nannostomus* and *Nannobrycon*, better known as the pencil fishes. These fish are found in South America, mainly in the Amazon region. They are quite shy and withdrawn, and must definitely be kept in a shoal. The larger the shoal, the more at home these fish will feel.

Nannobrycon eques *almost always swims with its head upwards and tail downwards.*

Myleus rubripinnis

During the day they can usually be found amongst the dense vegetation and they do not look for food until the evening. The typical characteristic of these two genera is that most of them swim with their heads pointing slightly upwards, so that they float diagonally in the water. This also immediately makes it clear what is on these fishes' menu: insects. In the aquarium they not only eat small live food but also dry food. Pencil fishes do not grow to large sizes, and their length averages between 4 and 6 centimetres. Since they are fairly sensitive to the water composition, they are not particularly suitable for aquarists who are beginners. The optimum water type for these fish should be rather acidic (pH 6) and soft water.

The **Serrasalmidae** *family*

This American salmonoid family includes fish which appear outwardly to be very similar. These shoaling fish virtually all have a flattened and disc-shaped body which is a silvery colour. They may seem alike, but their menu is very different. A number of species, including *Metynnis argenteus,* only eats vegetable food, while *Serrasal-*

mus natteri, the red piranha, is a real carnivore. Other species such as *Metynnis maculatus* and *Myleus rubripinnis* eat both vegetable food and small live food. All these species will need a large aquarium with plenty of space for swimming and water that is constantly in motion. They like to swim against the current. This family of fishes lives in South America in well-oxygenated, fast-flowing rivers and is not very good at coping with polluted water.

Distichodus sexfasciatus

African characins

The family of African characins *(Citharinidae)* differs quite starkly from most aquarium fish which come from the Americas. Most of the fish in this family are large shoaling fish which are not really suitable for aquaria. The vegetarian *Distichodos sexfasciatus* is a good example of the type. This species looks quite splendid when it is young, but as the fish grows older and larger, the striking colours gradually disappear and the fish become a practically monotone grey-brown. By that time they will also have eaten all the plants in the aquarium. In their country of origin, the Republic of Congo, this fish is a popular source of food, but there it can also grow to more than 1m in length. In the aquarium this shoaling fish will rarely exceed 30cm.

Family Alestidae

The family *Alestidae* includes a number of popular aquarium fish. The natural habitat of these fish is in Africa, particularly in the West, where they swim around actively in large shoals. The congo tetra *(Phenacogrammus interruptus)* is doubtless the best-known fish in this family. Males grow to about 8cm long, and the females remain a few centimetres smaller. The males are much more noticeable, not only because of their colouring, but also because of their longer fins. Congo tetra need a lot of space and must always be kept in a shoal. They like a current in the water, but do not like bright light. Floating plants and water plants with large, wispy leaves can be used to create a shadowy aquarium in which these fish will definitely feel at home. If

Hemigrammoptersius caudalis is a shoaling fish.

Ladigesia roloffi

Phenacogrammus interruptus

the bottom is also kept dark, their colours will show up better.

Congo tetra are mobile fish which usually occupy the middle zone. They are very peaceful and are not very well able to cope with aggression from other fish. They are not very demanding when it comes to feeding, and will eat both dry food and live food. They do have certain requirements as regards the water composition, preferring water which is rather acidic.

Another member of this family is *Hemigrammopetersius caudalis*. This shoaling fish grows to about 6cm in length and swims in the middle zone. If they are not kept in a shoal, these active and friendly fish hide amongst the vegetation and hardly show themselves at all.

The difference between the sexes is very easy to detect. The males have white spots on their fins, which are also much longer than those of the females. *Caudalis* only occurs in the Republic of Congo.

Another friendly fish, but much smaller than the species mentioned above, is *Ladigesia roloffi*. This species barely grows to 4cm in length. Its body is virtually transparant, with a golden sheen, and the fins are bright red. It can take some time before the young fish develop their mature colours. They are quite shy and frighten easily, and it is therefore better not to keep them together with large and rough or even intolerant types of fish. This is another species that likes rather soft, acidic water. If the aquarium water is too hard they will definitely fall ill.

The unusual patterning of Thayeria boehlkei *has led to its being nicknamed the 'hockeystick'.*

CHAPTER 9

Killifish

Killifish, or egg-laying tooth carps, are found in all the world's continents except Australia. The scientific name of this family of fishes is *Cyprinodontidae*. Many killifish are among the most colourful fish in existence, and due to their small size and quiet lifestyle they are very well suited to smaller aquaria. The killifish found most often are *Aphyosemion australe* and *Aphyosemion gardneri*, but *Epiplatys dageti* and *Epiplatys sexfasciatus* are also popular aquarium fish.

Aphyosemion australe, *variant*

The behaviour of killifish

Most killifish occupy the middle and top zones. Their diet consists of small flies and mosquitoes which have landed on the water surface. In the aquarium they also like to eat live food, and there are even some species which will not accept anything else, which means that keeping them is not easy. However there are many killifish which will eat dry food without difficulty, although it will have to be of a very high quality.

In the wild most killifish do not live in groups, but alone or as a pair. In the aquarium it is perfectly possible to keep several pairs together in a medium-sized aquarium as long as there is enough space for all the fish. Male fish will fight if the aquarium is only populated by three or four pairs, but if there are more than this, the aggressive behaviour among the males will soon disappear. It is therefore recommended either to keep these fish in a small aquarium as a pair, or to keep eight to ten pairs in a medium-sized aquarium. Killifish are relatively quiet fish which spend long periods of time resting completely still just below the water surface. When an insect lands on the water surface they come into action at lightning speed. In their enthusiasm they do sometimes jump out above the water surface.

Seasonal fish

Members of the killifish family have a reputation for being short-lived, but this actually only applies to a few species, the so-called seasonal

The males of almost all killifish tend to fight amongst themselves.

Nothobranchius patrizi *is a seasonal fish.*

fish. The African genus *Nothobranchius* and South American *Cynolebias* and *Pterolebias* are examples of these. They live in water which completely dries out during the dry season, so that the fish are doomed to die. Once they have emerged from the egg, they become sexually mature and reproduce extremely fast.

The eggs are laid in the bottom and covered with earth. They remain there, sometimes for months, well buried in the moist earth and therefore protected from drying out. When the rainy season begins, the area becomes flooded again and the eggs hatch. This brings the whole cycle back to the beginning.

If these are fish are kept in the aquarium they can grow older than is the case in nature. One noticeable feature of these fish is that they develop tremendously fast and greedily eat huge amounts. Their whole being is geared towards becoming sexually mature as quickly as possible and producing offspring. Since they eat so much they produce a correspondingly large quantity of excrement, which places a burden on the water composition in a small aquarium. A powerful motorised filter – which is so useful with gluttonous cichlids, who can make such a mess of their living environment – is completely unsuitable for these fish. They are not very good at coping with the strong flow in the water caused by such motorised filters. It is therefore best to change part of the aquarium water at least once every two weeks and preferably more often than that, and replace it with fresh water of the correct composition.

Aphyosemion gardneri

A killifish aquarium

Killifish are usually kept in an aquarium which has been specially set up for this type of fish. This is because they can be rather shy in the presence of other species. Killifish also make demands on the set up of the aquarium, which need not be particularly large. Virtually all killifish become withdrawn and their colours fade if they are kept in a brightly lit aquarium. A dimly lit aquarium is a better living environment for them. However, such twilight surroundings are not exactly ideal for most water plants, which actually need a lot of light in order to grow. Java moss, however, is one of the plant varieties which can still grow well when there is not much light. Due to this characteristic and due to the fact that this feathery-leafed, dark-coloured moss species provides a perfect laying substrate for the fish, java moss is widely used in killifish aquaria. The bottom should consist partly or entirely of peat dust.

Killifish like to hide near convoluted pieces of root wood. Finally, a solid leaf cover of floating plants will definitely help these fish to feel comfortable. Killifish have a reputation for only being able to survive in very soft and acidic water, but it has been found that most species do not have problems in water with a hardness of

Aphyosemon australe *is one of the most popular killifish.*

Nothobranchius rachovi *is a seasonal fish.*

The natural habitat of killifish

between 8° and 12°DH at a pH of about 6.5. The killifish from Europe and Central America will do better in water which is harder and has a more neutral acidity.

Not all killifish have to be kept in a special aquarium. *Aphyosemion gardneri* and *Epiplatys dageti*, for example, will also do well in a community aquarium, as long as there are sufficient refuges and as long as the other inhabitants leave them alone.

Cynolebias nigripinnis

The sub-family Rivulinae

The sub-family *Rivulinae* definitely includes the most popular killifish. The species belonging to the *Aphyosemion* and *Epiplatys* genera can regularly be found in aquarium centres.
Within this sub-family the sexes are usually very easy to distinguish. The males steal the show with their splendid colours and longer fins,

while the females are usually rather smaller and paler.

Within the *Aphysosemion* genus, *Aphyosemion australe*, also known as the Cape Lopez, and *Aphyosemion gardneri* are the best-known species. The males grow to about 6cm long,

Aplocheilus lineatus

Epiplatys dageti

African jungle, where the foliage is so dense and closely packed that sunlight barely penetrates to the shallow, slow-flowing streams strewn with dead leaves in which these fish are found.

The genus *Diapteron* also falls within the sub-family *Rivulinae*. These fish have many similarities with the *Aphyosemion* species.

Fish that belong to the *Nothobranchius* genus

Pachypanchax playfairii

while the females are usually rather smaller. Both species can be kept in a community aquarium, as long as the demands which these fish place on their environment are taken into account. They are colourful and friendly fish, which usually spend their time just below the surface of the water. Their natural biotope is the have a body shape which is rather different from that of most other killifish. They are rather taller, and their eyes are larger. One well-known species is *Nothobranchius rachovi*. These fish, which originate from Mozambique, grow to about 5cm long. They live on the African steppes in small pools which dry out completely during the dry season, and belong to the group of *seasonal fish.* They lay their eggs amongst dense foliage, near or on the bottom. There are few fish species whose sexes are as easy to determine as this one. Not only are the males much larger than the females, they are also striking in colour, while the females are virtually colourless.

Another seasonal fish which belongs to the sub-family *Rivulinae* is *Cynolebias nigripinnis.*

This attractive South American fish grows to about 6cm in length. Immediately after these fish emerge from the egg, their main activity is eating. They grow extremely fast, and within seven weeks they are fully grown and sexually mature.

Aphyosemion exiguum

Roloffia occidentalis

Rivulus xiphidius

The natural habitat of the Rivulus *species.*

Unfortunately they do not live long. In the wild they do not usually live more than seven months, but if they are well looked after they can live rather longer in the aquarium.

Fish belonging to the *Epiplatys* genus are real surface dwellers. Unlike many other fish in the same family they do very well in quiet community aquaria where the other inhabitants are not too aggressive or predatory. The water composition is not particularly important, although they have a preference for slightly acidic and rather soft water. *Epiplatys dageti* is sometimes thought to be similar in appearance to the pike, but this is quite misleading. There are two different types: *Epiplatys dageti dageti* is quite colourless, with the exception of a number of black transverse bands on its body, while *Epiplatys dageti monroviae* is conspicuous on account of its bright red throat. This species, which grows to about 6cm long, is also the most popular. They will readily eat dry food, although

they will certainly appreciate some live food
from time to time. One typical characteristic is
that these fish are found both in areas which are
left high and dry during the dry season and in
water where the water level is not much affected
by the seasons. They have managed to adapt
successfully to both habitats.

Other well-known aquarium fish which are
included in the sub-family *Rivulunae* are *Aplocheilus lineatus, Aplocheilus panchax* and
Aplocheilus dayi. The *lineatus* is most often
kept as an aquarium fish. This species grows to
about 10cm long and is not very friendly to its
neighbours, unlike so many other killifish. Its
diet consists almost exclusively of solid live food
such as insects, mosquito larvae and small
fish. These fish mainly live in the top zone and
because they become quite active from time to
time they will definitely need a rather larger
aquarium than most other killifish. Their place
of origin is South-East Asia, including India and
Sri Lanka, where they live in slow-flowing
shallow water along riverbanks and amongst the
vegetation. Due to the sunshine, the water
temperature in these waters can rise quickly, but
in the aquarium this fish prefers a temperature of
about 23°C. Because they are so aggressive, they
are almost always kept either as a pair in a

Diapteron abanicum

Aphyosemion bitaeniatum 'Lagos'

special aquarium or together with larger, robust
species.

Another intolerant species which grows to about
the same size is *Pachypanchax playfairii.* These

Aphyosemion sjoestedti

fish form a territory within which they will not tolerate any other fish at all. Their diet consists of insects and their larvae, but they will also eat small fish. They are found on islands near the east coast of Africa, such as Madagascar and the Seychelles.

The sub-family Fundulinae

There is actually only one aquarium fish in this sub-family which is regularly imported, and that is *Lucania goodei*. This friendly and lively fish grows to about 5cm long and originally comes

Lucania goodei

Above: the biotope of Procatopodinae.

Lucania goodei, *the fish above is the male.*

from the Southern United States. Since the climate there is pleasant but certainly not tropical, this fish can very easily be kept in an unheated aquarium. It is even recommended to allow the water temperature to fall by a few degrees during the winter, since this will encourage the fish to lay their eggs when they see the first rays of sun-shine and feel the water temperature rise again.

Lucania goodei is not a difficult fish to keep. They like live food, but will accept dry food as well. The aquarium does not need to be big, but it must provide refuges for the fish, such as water plants and root wood. Fish like these should ideally be kept as a number of pairs. The difference between males and females is not difficult to detect. The males are larger, they have more colour, particularly on their fins, and their fins are more robust. These fish can be kept together with others which make similar demands on the water temperature, but they are not suitable as company for slower or fragile species. When they get older they can sometimes be intolerant towards their neighbours.

Procatopodinae

The genus *Procatopodinae* is characterised by the fact that the fish have luminous eyes. They are found in Africa, where they live both in small pools in the savanna and in larger lakes. Fishes in this genus have no difficulty with a more or less brightly lit aquarium, because they are used to it in their natural biotope. They are shoaling fish and they must always be kept in a group of at least eight to twelve. The largest species in this genus is *Lamprichthys tanganicanus*, a particularly attractive fish which can grow to a length of 15cm.

CHAPTER 10

Other fish

In addition to the large and well-known fish families which have already been discussed, there is still a number of very interesting families which more than merit closer study.

Erpetoichthys ornatipinnis

Freshwater ray

Freshwater rays can actually only be kept in an aquarium specially set up for the species. This is not because they will endanger the lives of the other fish, but because most fish like to have some plants in the aquarium which will prevent these fish from swimming. The best known freshwater ray is the South American *Potamotrygon motoro*. This fish grows to about 30cm long and lives almost exclusively on or near the bottom. Since they like to bury themselves in the sand, these fish need to be given an opportunity to do this. A gravel bottom is definitely unsuitable. They eat small live food such as tubifex and mosquito larvae, and small pieces of fish and meat will also be accepted.

Butterfly fish

The butterfly fish family *(Pantodontidae)* is the smallest family of fish known to us. In fact it only contains one species, *Pantodon buchholzi*. This African fish grows to about 15cm long and lives in small streams and lakes in the jungle. It spends most of the day resting. At dusk it goes out hunting for insects and their larvae. The huge pectoral fins and the whole build of this fish demonstrate that it does not always stay in the water. It is a good jumper, and can make huge leaps out of the water for a tasty morsel. If these fish are kept in an aquarium a cover will be needed to make sure they do not jump out of the aquarium. Butterfly fish are solitary creatures. They do not feel the need for others of

The freshwater ray hides in the sandy bottom when he feels threatened.

The butterfly fish lives almost exclusively on insects and their larvae.

their own kind to keep them company. It is best to keep them as solitary fish together with others larger than themselves, because they can move very suddenly and will not hesitate to chase and devour smaller fish.

In captivity they will sometimes eat dry food, but mostly live food such as mosquito larvae and insects. Their way of life makes these fish ideal for a paludarium.

Gobiidae

This family mainly consists of sea fish, but there are also a number of species which are found in brackish and fresh water. The best known goby is no doubt the bumblebee *(Brachygobius xanthozona)*, but the mudskipper, which lives partly on land, is also a member of this large family of fish. The bumblebee, which needs a warm environment, grows to about 4 or 5cm

The bumble bee is a small, quiet fish with a preference for brackish water.

long and lives a quiet and withdrawn life in a small, protected territory. These are not the easiest fish to keep in an aquarium, since they do best in brackish water and can rarely be persuaded to eat dry food.

Stigmatogobius sadanundio

be kept in a community aquarium with other fish which appreciate a little salt in the water, such as the sailfin molly and the black molly. *Stigmatogobius sadanundio* is a quiet fish which tends to keep to itself, does not trouble the other fish and needs plenty of opportunities to take refuge.

Polypteridae

One member of the bumblebee's family, *Stigmatogobius sadanundio*, is rather easier to satisfy with regard to the water composition. This fish will do better if a few spoonfuls of sea salt are added to the aquarium water, but it can also survive for a time in pure fresh water. They are not very good swimmers, and usually stay near to the bottom nearly all the time. These gobies can

In the hottest parts of Africa we find the family *Polypteridae*. This is a family of predatory fish whose body shape makes them look very much like eels. They have a deformed air bladder which acts as a type of lung, and they must therefore be able to come up to the surface regularly for air. Various species within this family are suitable for aquaria, but *Erpetoichthys ornatipinnis* is the best-known of all. This fish grows to more than 35cm in length and can

Rhinogobius wui is a member of the goby family.

Erpetoichthys ornatipinnis

be accommodated in a large aquarium. Due to its predatory character these fish should be kept together with large cichlids. They are rarely seen during the day. They lie basking amongst rocks or under a piece of wood until night falls. Only then do they become active and go out looking for food. This fish is a solitary creature which does not need others of its kind to feel comfortable. Its diet consists of small fish, pieces of mussel, shrimps, earthworms and pieces of beef heart.

Mormyrids (Mormyridae)

Mormyrids are a separate group of fish. They are noticeable because of their unusual body shape and they have an electrical organ at the base of their tail which enables them to find their way in cloudy water. Their brain is relatively large and these are therefore suspected to be very intelligent fish.

The best known mormyrid is definitely *Gnathonemus petersii*, the elephant fish. This fish can grow to about 20cm long, depending on the space available. These are definitely solitary fish, and they occupy a territory close to the bottom. They stay hidden during the day and become

Gobiopterus chuno

It is suspected that Gnathonomeus petersii *is a very intelligent fish, since it has a relatively large brain capacity.*

active at nightfall when they go out looking for food. They use their proboscidiform mouth to search around the bottom for small shrimps and worms, but in the aquarium they will also eat dry food.

Elephant fish tend to keep to themselves and leave other fish alone.

Puffer fish

Most puffer fish *(Tetraodontidae)* are sea dwellers. Only a few species are found in brackish and fresh water. The principal feature of these fish is that they can puff themselves up if they are under threat, and a number of them are even poisonous. The puffer fish which are sold in aquarium centres are actually all brackish water fish with one exception, *Tetraodon biocellatus.* Brackish water is precisely halfway between

Puffer fish love snails. They spend almost the whole day searching for them.

fresh water and seawater. Brackish water fish usually live in coastal areas where seawater and water from rivers meet.

Puffer fish are usually peaceful fish with a typical

way of moving. Their diet consists almost exclusively of snails. Their mouths are so hard and strong that they can crack open a snail's shell very quickly. If there are enough snails in the aquarium, a puffer fish will not need any other food.

Once the stocks are gone, however, and that will happen quite quickly at the rate these fish eat, they will have to be given extra mussels and earthworms. If a puffer fish does not get enough to eat, the fish population in the aquarium will not be safe either. Puffer fish should therefore only be kept together with robust and fast-swimming species, and most puffer fish simply should not be kept in a community aquarium at all. Most brackish and freshwater puffer fish grow to 6 or 7cm.

Osteoglossidae

The predators in the *Osteoglossidae* family are found in South America, where their appearance will cause many fish to flee. They are very large.

Puffer fish

Osteoglossum bicirrhosum is found in South America and can grow to 1m or more.

Pseudomugil furcata

Following pages: Melanotaenia herbertaxelrodi, one of the most spectacularly coloured rainbow fish.

The best known is *Osteoglossum bicirrhosum*, which is more than a metre long. It is not always easy to keep several fish of this species in the same aquarium, since they do not usually get on outside the mating season. They have not yet been bred in the aquarium, but in the wild it has been observed that the males keep the eggs in their mouth until they hatch.

From that time onwards the fry can already look after themselves fairly well. This large predator has a diet consisting almost exclusively of smaller fish.

Mastacembelus *has a mobile proboscis which it uses to search for food.*

Spiny eels

Spiny eels or *Mastacembelidae* are found in Africa and China and in some parts of Asia. The spiny eel is a remarkable creature altogether. Due to its elongated shape and the elegant way it moves it is immediately noticed. It also has an unusually shaped mouth, ending in a very mobile proboscis, which the spiny eel uses to look for food. Spiny eels are active at night. During the day they like to bury themselves, and only appear again at dusk. When danger threatens they also take refuge under the surface of the bottom.

Spiny eels are real carnivores. They eat small worms, insects and their larvae, but small fish are also on the menu. Some types will also eat dry food on occasion. This species should be kept together with other and definitely larger species. Spiny eels are solitary creatures, and if

Melanotaenia macullochi

more than one is kept together this will often lead to problems. The size of the aquarium depends on the species. There are some very small spiny eels which only grow to 10cm long, but there are other species which grow to 1m or longer.

Rainbow fish

Rainbow fish *(Melanotaeniidae)* are only found in Australia and the nearby islands of Asia. They are robust, often brightly coloured fish, and most of them can grow to a reasonable length. As their body shape suggests, they are strong and fast swimmers. In an aquarium these active creatures will definitely need plenty of space. They like mineral-rich, clear water with a strong current. The aquarium should be well lit, and they will even appreciate some direct sunlight. Rainbow fish are usually kept in a specially set up aquarium which is specifically suited to their natural living environment. In this type of aquarium the bottom covering should consist of sand, and there should definitely be some peripheral vegetation in an aquarium containing rainbow fish. In a tank like this you will not have to wait long for the first eggs. Most rainbow fish are very colourless and boring as young fish, and it can take quite some time before the spectacular colours to which the fish owes its name have fully developed.

Silversides

There are only a few freshwater species in the silversides family *(Atherinidae)*. One of these is a well-known aquarium fish, the Celebes rainbow fish. These decorative and mobile shoaling fish mainly spend their time in the middle and

Melanotaenia lacistrus

top zones. Due to their active lifestyle they definitely need plenty of space for swimming, but feathery-leaved peripheral vegetation should also be available. This species is good for keeping in a community aquarium and will do well in both soft and harder water, although soft water made slightly more acidic will more closely imitate the conditions in which these fish are found in the wild. The difference between the males and females is clearly visible. The males have longer fin rays and much more pigment than the rather drab females. Celebes rainbow fish are only found on the island of Celebes and grow to around 7cm long.

Bedotia geayi *is a silverside.*

Thelmatherina ladigesi *is found only on Celebes, and it is a peaceful and mobile shoaling fish.*

Index

Photographic

acknowledgements

All photographs were taken by Norbert
Dadaniak and Reinhard Lutje.

Additional material was provided by:
Sera MbgH, Heinsberg, Germany;
Otto Roth, Seeheim, Lüdenscheid;
Gerd Schreiber, Aqua Fauna aquarium
association;
Esther J.J. Verhoef-Verhallen.